D1066135

ASK
SUZE®

. . . ABOUT MUTUAL FUNDS

AND ANNUITIES

ALSO BY SUZE ORMAN

You've Earned It, Don't Lose It
Suze Orman's Financial Guidebook
The 9 Steps to Financial Freedom
The Courage to Be Rich
The Road to Wealth
The Laws of Money, The Lessons of Life
The Money Book for the Young, Fabulous & Broke
Women & Money

Riverhead Books
a member of
Penguin Group (USA) Inc.
New York
2007

ASK SUZE®

...ABOUT MUTUAL FUNDS AND ANNUITIES

SUZE ORMAN

RIVERHEAD BOOKS
a member of
Penguin Group (USA) Inc.
375 Hudson Street
New York, NY 10014

ISBN 978-1-59448-965-5

Printed in the United States of America
1   3   5   7   9   10   8   6   4   2

Book design by Deborah Kerner and Claire Vaccaro

ASK SUZE®

. . . ABOUT MUTUAL FUNDS AND ANNUITIES

THE GOOD, THE BAD, AND THE UGLY

When you put money into a mutual fund instead of buying shares of individual stocks, you are essentially hiring a trained professional to pick your stocks for you. In good, active funds, the fund manager is trained to locate the best-performing stocks of the kind that you want to invest in. There are a lot of mutual funds around these days—as many as 8,000, by some estimates. There are mutual funds for people interested in investing in small companies, large companies, sectors of the economy such as technology or health services, specific foreign regions or countries, environmentally sensitive companies, and the broadest array of companies under the umbrella of one big, diversified fund. There are also mutual funds that charge you too much in sales charges and annual fees, don't perform as well as they should, and generally slow you down on the road to financial freedom. This chapter will show you how to stay away from those. It's impossible to cover every type of mutual fund available. But it's not hard to grasp the fundamentals of mutual funds—their basic terms and operating principles. The most important things to look for are good management, a long history of good performance, and very low fees and charges. And once you understand the general idea, you open your investment options wide. The questions and answers in this chapter will provide you with a working knowledge of the fundamentals of this often excellent investment option.

MUTUAL FUND BASICS

What is a mutual fund?
A mutual fund is an investment vehicle that can be compared to a basket filled with stocks. You and many other investors pool your money to buy a portion of everything that's in the basket, which has been assembled with an eye toward meeting certain investment goals. What those goals are depends on the particular mutual fund. For example, one mutual fund might aim toward growth in the value of the stocks in the fund, and another might try to generate income from dividends. Every mutual fund has a clearly defined investment objective, as well as guidelines that determine how the objective may be achieved.

Who decides how to invest all this money?
Each mutual fund is run by a portfolio manager (or a team of managers) who chooses the stocks in the fund and makes other investment decisions. The fund manager decides which stocks to buy and when, and also decides if and when those stocks should be sold. The fund manager assembles a portfolio of stocks that he or she thinks will outperform the market—that is, will generate more growth or income than other, similar

groups of stocks—with an eye toward giving investors the best return on their investment. A fund manager can make or break a fund, since he or she makes all the critical investment decisions regarding it.

What exactly am I buying when I buy a mutual fund?

You are buying actual shares in that particular fund. A share represents a unit of ownership in the mutual fund, just as a share of stock in a publicly traded company represents partial ownership of that company. The share price of a mutual fund is sometimes referred to as net asset value.

What does net asset value mean?

The net asset value, or NAV, is the share price of the fund. At the end of each day, the entire value of the portfolio of stocks and/or bonds, less any expenses and/or liabilities, is added up. That total is divided by the number of shares outstanding. This is the net asset value.

Why would I buy a mutual fund instead of buying individual stocks?

Mutual funds allow you to diversify your investments quickly and with minimal risk. Let's say you have $1,000 to invest. When you put it in a mutual fund, you are buying a small slice of a very big pie that can contain hundreds of different stocks. Let's imagine that one company whose stocks are held within the mutual fund goes belly-up. As a result, the price of your mutual fund shares may temporarily drop in value slightly, but this wouldn't be a financial crisis for the mutual fund or for you. If, on the other hand, you had invested $1,000 in shares of that individual stock, you would lose all your money. Intelligent diversification—that is, spreading your money out among a variety of investments—is the key to being a smart investor. With small amounts of money, a mutual fund is a great way to achieve diversification.

Are you saying that only people with small sums of money are candidates for buying mutual funds?
Certainly not! People with large sums of money buy shares of mutual funds, too, because they like the fact that a trained portfolio manager is making the decisions about what and when to buy and sell. For fund investors, the only decision to make is which mutual fund to buy. Once you have purchased a mutual fund, the only *other* decision you will have to make is when to sell your shares. From the time you buy until the time you sell, your money is in the hands of the portfolio manager. Of course, choosing a mutual fund is not easy. I'll have much more to say about this later.

What if there is an enormous drop in the stock market and practically everything loses value? Will diversification still protect me?
If the market as a whole drops in value, your mutual fund—despite its diversification among a number of stocks—will drop in value, too. When, in a bear market, the majority of stocks fall, diversifying won't keep you from participating in the losses everyone experiences, but it may prevent your losses from becoming greater than the average loss. Bad times require commitment. If you are willing to weather a bear market, history has shown that the market will likely rise again.

Are there mutual funds that make money in a bear market?

Yes. There are all kinds of mutual funds, including those—known as "bear market" or "foul weather" funds—that actually perform best in bear markets.

How long does a bear market last?

Well, there is no way to know for sure, but in the past, bear markets typically have lasted between six months and two years, with the norm being between six and eighteen months.

Are all managed mutual funds diversified among hundreds of stocks?

No. Some mutual funds own hundreds of stocks, and others own only 20 or 30 stocks. According to Securities and Exchange Commission (SEC) rules, a so-called "diversified" mutual fund is required to invest in at least 16 companies. (A mutual fund is also prohibited from owning more than 25 percent of any one company.) Even with these regulations, mutual funds have plenty of discretion.

Is there an ideal number of stocks a mutual fund should have?

The best actively managed funds may have between 25 and 100 stocks in their portfolios. Very large funds—those with billions of dollars to invest—often have to overdiversify into hundreds of stocks in an effort to allocate all the money people have invested in them. Alternatively, some funds have too few holdings (this is much rarer than too many), which exposes investors to the extra risk of inadequate diversification.

Once I buy a mutual fund, am I ever allowed to take some of the money back out?

Of course. It's your money. You can sell all or any portion of your shares at any time through your mutual fund company, a broker or discount broker, or even an online broker. (Most mutual fund companies and brokerage firms offer an 800 number that investors can call to liquidate shares.) However, if your fund share price has gone down, you might not get what you paid for your shares.

What is the minimum initial amount I must invest in a mutual fund?

Most funds require an initial investment of $500 to $1,000 if the investment is made as part of an individual retirement account (IRA), and $2,500 to $3,000 outside of a retirement account. Vanguard, for example, requires a minimum $3,000 initial investment to open a fund account. But if you open an IRA using Vanguard's STAR mutual fund, the minimum falls to $1,000. Most mutual fund companies, or families, work in more or less the same way, although a few good ones will let you invest with minimums as low as $50 to $250. These include T. Rowe Price, (800) 638-5660; Managers Funds, (800) 548-4539; and TIAA, (800) 223-1200. Many mutual funds waive the minimum investment if you sign up for automatic monthly withdrawals, in which the fund takes $50 to $100 a month from a checking account and invests it.

What are mutual fund families?

"Fund family" is the cozy name given to a group of mutual funds that are managed by one company, such as Fidelity, T. Rowe Price, or Vanguard. The fund family's individual funds are under the same umbrella, but tend to have different investment objectives. Within some fund families, you can move your money from one fund to another without hassle or expense.

Some of the great fund families are:

Fidelity Investments (800) 544-9797 *www.fidelity.com*
T. Rowe Price (800) 638-5660 *www.troweprice.com*
Vanguard (800) 662-2739 *www.vanguard.com*

TYPES OF MUTUAL FUNDS

It's crucial to know a mutual fund's investment objective (*and* its performance record, but more about that later) in order to know whether that fund is right *for you*. By "right," I mean suited to an investor of your age, your income, your tax status, and your short- and long-term financial goals, including goals for your children (for example, college tuition, graduate school, or wedding expenses), and your retirement plans. Whatever your financial profile, there is probably a mutual fund that will help you achieve your dreams.

How many kinds of mutual funds are there?

There are hundreds of kinds of funds, each with a slightly different objective, but in general, mutual funds are divided into four large groups: growth funds; balanced funds; income, or bond, funds; and money-market funds. (In this book, we'll cover stock funds, such as growth and balanced funds. For more information on bond funds and money-market funds, please see the later sections of this book.) Each of the four groups can be, and is, divided into many subgroups, including mutual funds that are variously described as managed funds, index funds, exchange-traded funds, load and no-load funds, open-end and closed-end funds, and on and on.

GROWTH FUNDS

What is a growth fund?

Growth funds emphasize adding to your investment capital by choosing investments that will increase in market value over time. Growth funds invest in companies that are likely to increase their annual earnings and/or their market share. Such funds do not invest primarily in stocks of companies that pay a dividend—meaning money that is paid to shareholders out of earnings, which growth companies tend to reinvest in their businesses. If you are able to let your money remain invested for ten years or more, do not need income from your investments now, and if growth of your investment capital is your objective, good growth funds can be an excellent choice.

There are many kinds of growth funds, including aggressive growth funds, value funds, blended funds, international stock funds, global funds, emerging-market funds, sector funds, socially responsible funds, large-capitalization funds, mid-capitalization funds, and small-capitalization funds.

What is an aggressive growth fund?

Many growth funds are made up of stocks of large, well-established companies whose earnings are growing rapidly. An aggressive growth fund is made up of stocks that the portfolio manager believes have greater-than-ordinary potential for growth and that, as a result, tend to be somewhat more speculative and move up and down in price faster than the overall market. An aggressive growth fund may bypass conventional blue-chip stocks, concentrating instead on less-well-known securities in an attempt to make larger profits if and when the stocks take off. The usual trade-off applies, of course: The higher the rate of return you seek, the higher the risk. This is *not* the best kind of fund for people whose objective is to keep their money safe in the short term.

What is a value fund?

Value funds tend to invest in large- and medium-size companies whose stock prices are below those of average similar companies in relation to such factors as earnings and book value—in other words, whose stocks offer value for the price. These stocks tend to pay above-average dividends.

What is a blended fund?

Blended funds invest in both growth and value stocks.

What is an international fund?

International funds invest in foreign stocks and bonds. Some international funds invest in specific geographic regions, such as the Pacific Rim; others put all their investments into a single country, for example, Chile.

What is the difference between an international fund and a global fund?

International funds invest only abroad; global funds invest in securities in both the United States and abroad.

Given the volatile state of the world today, international funds sound risky. Are they?

Well, the world is a pretty big place. It's not volatile everywhere, not by a long shot. Some countries (and investments) are riskier than others—and what you might call risky, another investor might call a walk around the block. Besides, if your mutual fund invests in several countries, the risk to you, the shareholder, is reduced. For example, when the market in Europe falls, the market in Asia may rise—sometimes in reaction to that falling European market. If your fund invests in only one country, the chances for a total loss—or, for that matter, an enormous gain—are greater. However, for most of us, diversification, whether we are investing here in the United States, abroad, or both, is always important.

What is an emerging-market fund?

An emerging-market fund invests in developing regions of the world, such as Latin America or Eastern Europe. ("Developing," incidentally, is a duffel bag of a word, containing every kind of society that's not destitute or affluent.) These stocks are generally inexpensive, either in relation to their markets or to the stocks of other comparable companies in other countries. They can be extremely volatile. Remember the meltdown in Southeast Asian markets and Brazil's financial woes? Volatility is one of the potential hazards for the investor in an emerging-market fund. Still, there are some extraordinary bargains in these funds, too.

What is a sector fund?

A sector fund is also known as a specialty fund. These are mutual funds that invest in the stocks of one industry—such as telecommunications, utilities, chemicals, precious metals, or pharmaceuticals. Some specialty funds are riskier than others, but the risk depends on a particular fund's investments.

What is a socially responsible fund?

Socially responsible funds typically avoid investing in companies that may cause harm to people, animals, or the environment. There's such a vast number of securities out there, some investors reason, that surely it's possible to make money without damaging the planet or the creatures on it. So most socially responsible mutual funds do not invest in tobacco, nuclear energy, or armaments companies. Nor do they buy shares of companies that have a history of discriminating against women or minorities, mistreating their employees, or polluting the environment. You can find a comprehensive listing of socially responsible funds on the Internet, at *www.socialinvest.org*. My favorite is the Domini Social Equity fund.

What is the difference between large-cap, mid-cap, and small-cap mutual funds?

These designations refer to companies of a certain size, "cap" being shorthand for capitalization. Broadly speaking, small-cap refers to a corporation whose capitalization (or market value) falls below $1.5 billion. Mid-cap refers to companies whose capitalization runs between $1.5 billion and $12 billion. Large-cap companies have capitalization of $12 billion or more. A large-cap mutual fund invests in companies with large capitalization; a mid-cap fund buys stock in mid-cap companies; and so on.

What is the difference between a large-cap growth fund, a large-cap value fund, and a large-cap blend fund?

A large-cap growth fund concentrates its investments in well-known, well-managed companies with proven track records of growth in share price and a history of outperforming the markets. They pay out relatively small dividends, if any; they invest for long-term growth. A large-cap value fund, on the other hand, generally focuses its investments on large companies that the fund manager believes are undervalued and that the rest of the investing world will someday recognize as winners.

A large-cap blend fund combines these two financial strategies, investing in both growth stocks and value stocks.

Mid-cap and small-cap companies also use these classifications. A small-cap growth mutual fund will invest in new or smaller companies that are growing rapidly and that are typically focused on some up-to-the-minute industry, such as biotechnology. In general, fund managers purchase shares early in the game and hold them for a long time. A small-cap value fund will concentrate its investments on better-established though under-recognized small companies. A mid-cap or small-cap blend fund combines these two investment styles.

INCOME FUNDS

The objective of income funds is, of course, to provide regular current income to investors. Income funds commonly invest in bonds or high-dividend-paying stocks, and accordingly, they are not as likely as growth funds to make you a lot of money. Income funds pay the investor dividends and/or interest, typically on a monthly basis. Bond or income funds are popular with retirees who have seen their money grow during their working years and now want a monthly income that they can count on. To investors in bond or income funds, regular income is more important than the growth or possible loss of principal. For a more thorough discussion of bond funds, Treasury bill funds, CDs, money-market funds, and other income funds, please see the later sections of this book.

BALANCED FUNDS

What is a balanced fund?
A balanced fund is a marriage of a mutual fund that deals

exclusively in stocks and one that deals exclusively with bonds, mixing the two, usually fifty-fifty. Balanced funds are less risky than stock funds, but in a bear market they can be a little more precarious than bond funds.

There are two basic types of balanced mutual funds:

- Traditional balanced funds invest in a fairly stable mix of stocks, bonds, and money-market instruments in an effort to provide growth, income, and conservation of capital. They are considered to be a relatively conservative investment option. Their net asset values will fluctuate along with the movements of the financial markets, but they tend to experience fewer price swings than a portfolio made up entirely of stocks.

- Asset-allocation funds also invest in a mix of stocks, bonds, and money-market instruments. However, as market conditions change, these funds switch the percentage of their holdings in each asset class according to the performance (or expected performance) of that class. As a result, asset-allocation funds tend to be more volatile than traditional balanced funds.

OPEN- AND CLOSED-END FUNDS

What is an open-end fund?
Most mutual funds are open-end. This means that there is no limit to the number of shares that the fund can issue and sell—so the growth of the fund, in terms of investment dollars, is open-ended. An open-end fund's price is referred to as a net asset value (NAV) rather than a price per share (even though price per share is essentially what an NAV is).

So there is no limit to the amount of money investors can put into an open-end mutual fund?

Correct. But a fund manager may sometimes close the fund to new investors once the fund has taken in as much money as is manageable. (Investors who are already part of the fund can usually continue to invest money in it.)

What's a closed-end fund?

In a closed-end mutual fund, the number of shares available for sale to the public is established at the outset. After those shares have been sold, the fund is closed and new investors can buy into the fund only if someone who owns shares wants to sell them. A closed-end fund is priced and traded just like a stock. Shares are usually sold on the American Stock Exchange.

Closed-end funds are far less common than open-end funds. When people talk generally about mutual funds, such as those that are commonly offered in 401(k) and 403(b) retirement plans, they're talking about open-end funds.

MANAGED MUTUAL FUNDS vs. INDEXED MUTUAL FUNDS

Most mutual funds are managed funds—managed, that is, by an individual (or team) who decides what to buy and sell with the money the investors have deposited into the fund. Index funds, sometimes called passive funds, have managers too, but they simply buy the entire index that the fund is duplicating, such as the Standard & Poor's 500 Index.

MANAGED MUTUAL FUNDS

What do managed-fund managers look for in the companies they invest in?

Successfully picking a stock involves intuition and knowledge informed by research. Fund managers usually track the market in a number of ways that include, for example, scrutinizing price trends. Has the company in question shown a decent upward price trend? What about the industry involved? Is the U.S. economy in a recession, or have interest rates declined? Either situation can influence which kinds of stock the fund manager elects to invest in.

Most fund managers do hands-on research, too, and analysts within their companies typically advise them. They want to understand and monitor the goals of the companies in which they are thinking of buying stock. They try to determine a company's commitment to research and development. Does the company have a product in the pipeline that can't lose? Has the company been profitable for a number of years? What factors contributed to its winning streak?

Does the mutual fund manager have to inform me whenever he buys or sells something? And do I have to pay a commission when he does?

If you had a financial adviser at a full-service brokerage firm like Merrill Lynch, he or she usually would have to consult you before making any transactions, and you would probably have to pay a commission whenever you authorized him or her to buy or sell anything. This is not the case in a mutual fund, where the manager has free rein over the money in the fund and you're not charged an *individual* commission when transactions are made. (Transactions do cost you, however, both terms of yearly return and in end-of-the-year taxes, but more about that later.) Before you purchase shares of your fund, you will receive a prospectus and reports outlining the mutual fund's activities, but you're not notified of day-to-day changes. By buying shares in the fund, you have placed your trust in the fund manager. (Once you buy shares, you'll receive regular statements of your account's activity, and quarterly reports for the fund.)

Before you buy into a managed mutual fund, it's wise to check how long the manager has been in charge. Is the current manager responsible for a fund's terrific track record? Or has that person moved on, leaving someone new and relatively untested at the helm? It's the *manager's* track record you want to know, not the fund's. Ultimately, the fund manager is responsible for the fund's success.

INDEXED MUTUAL FUNDS

Why do so many people buy index funds?

Over many years, index funds have outperformed almost 85 percent of all managed mutual funds. In the late 90s, when the whole stock market was rising, many people made the greatest returns through investing in the S&P index funds, and an index fund is an easy way to invest. An index fund simply buys all the stocks in the relevant index, for example, the Standard & Poor's 500, and no one has to worry about the fund's manager leaving. In fact, one key to the better-than-average return on index funds is they cost so little to operate.

EXCHANGE-TRADED FUNDS

Exchange-traded funds (ETFs) are relatively recent investment vehicles, and they are definitely worth looking into when you're thinking about investing in mutual funds. They even have some advantages over index funds.

What are exchange-traded funds (ETFs)?

Exchange-traded funds (ETFs) combine the features of a mutual fund with those of a stock. Like mutual funds, ETFs track either an index of the broad stock market or bond market, stock industry sector, or international stock. ETFs move up or down as the stocks or bonds on the index they are tracking move. Yet ETFs trade like stocks that you can buy and sell throughout the trading day, which you cannot do with mutual funds.

What exactly am I buying when I buy an ETF? Am I buying a stock or a mutual fund?

When you buy an ETF, you are not buying shares of a stock or shares of a mutual fund. You are buying units of ownership in a trust that holds shares of the stocks or bonds tracked by a particular index, such as the S&P 500, in almost exact proportion to the weighting of the stocks on that index. In this way, an ETF is like an index fund, since you are buying the composition of the entire index. Because of this, an ETF offers a level of diversification that would be difficult for you to achieve on your own or through outright ownership of individual stocks, yet it trades and behaves like an individual stock. So you can buy and sell your shares during regular market hours, and there is no minimum investment amount as there is in many mutual funds.

What are the main differences between an ETF and a mutual fund?

In an ETF you can buy and sell the ETF while the markets are trading. In a mutual fund you can only get the closing price of that fund for that day regardless of what time you put your order in. So if something happens during the day and you want to sell your ETF immediately, you can do so—but that is not true with a mutual fund. Also, ETFs usually do not have end-of-the-year capital-gains distributions like mutual funds do. So if you are investing outside of a retirement account, this is important for you to take into consideration. Also, ETFs can be bought share by share, and there is no minimum investment, as there can be with many mutual funds. Bottom line: ETFs can be thought of as the modern-day mutual fund that brings you the best of both—stocks that allow you to buy or sell at any time, and the diversification and low costs of many mutual funds.

A friend told me I should look into iShares. What is the difference between an ETF and an iShare?

iShares are a group of ETFs advised and marketed by Barclays Global Investors. iShares are structured as open-end mutual funds. They really are the same exact thing, or a branded name of ETFs.

What are the risks of investing in ETFs?

It depends on the type of ETF that you purchase. Equity-based exchange-traded funds have risks similar to stocks and/

or equity mutual funds, so they will have market risk, while fixed-income-based ETFs have risks similar to a bond fund.

What are fixed-income ETFs?

Fixed-income ETFs track bond market indexes. Fixed-income ETFs tend to be more stable than equity ETFs because the bond markets are often less volatile than the stock markets. Please note that although I said *tend to be,* there are times that the bond market can be very volatile, as was the case in a seven-week period in the year 2003 when we saw a 150 basis point swing.

Do ETFs have a maturity date like a bond?

Technically, yes, although that date is more than 100 years in the future and so probably won't affect you.

Do equity ETFs pay dividends?

The units provide quarterly cash dividend distributions based on the accumulated dividends paid by the stocks held in the ETF trust minus an annual expense ratio and management fees ranging from .10 percent to more than 1.00 percent of principal to cover trust expenses. Please note, however, that the dividend is very, very low, so you can't count on them for income. This investment is usually for growth, and growth alone.

Do fixed-income ETFs pay dividends?

Yes. Dividends for fixed-income ETFs are distributed on a monthly basis, similar to bond mutual funds.

How can I buy an ETF?

ETFs are traded on the American Stock Exchange, the New York Stock Exchange, and the NASDAQ. They can be bought or sold through a broker or online throughout the trading day in the same manner as common stocks. The shares trade in minimum increments and, as with common stocks, there is a typical spread between the bid (what buyers are willing to pay) and asked price (what the sellers are asking for).

Am I better off buying an ETF or a managed mutual fund?

That depends on which managed mutual fund you want to buy. In general, ETFs have very low management fees and minimal stock turnover; in essence, they are just an index mutual fund sold as a stock, and in the past they, like index funds, have outperformed the vast majority of actively managed funds.

Am I better off buying an ETF or an index fund?

The answer will depend on how much money you have to invest and if you are investing inside or outside a retirement account, as well as how often you expect to invest. Many of the good index funds require a high initial deposit ($1,000–$3,000) to open an account. This is not true of ETFs. If you like, you can buy one share of an ETF, which could cost you as little as $25. Also, outside a retirement account, ETFs have an advantage, taxwise, over both managed funds and index funds. With ETFs, there usually is not an end-of-the-year capital-gains tax distribution, as there is with mutual funds. Please note: Even index funds, which don't buy and sell the stocks they hold as often as do managed funds, can have an end-of-the-year capital-gains distribution.

If you plan to dollar cost average into your chosen investment, adding a small sum of money to it every month, you would probably be better off in a no-load index fund; in many such funds, when you invest regularly and directly, the minimum initial deposit is reduced and there are no transaction costs. If you were to buy ETFs every month, the commission costs, even at just $10 per trade online, would seriously cut into your ability to profit. On the other hand, the annual expenses for ETFs are somewhat less than the expenses of many index funds.

Are ETFs easier to buy and sell than index funds?

Overall, they are. ETFs are traded in the same manner as stocks, so you can get price quotes and make trades anytime during the day. You can also designate the exact price that you are willing to pay (using a limit order). You can't do this with a mutual fund; because a fund's net asset value (the equivalent of share price) is calculated only once a day, you always get the closing price on the day your order for shares is placed. The ability to buy or sell ETFs at any time during the market day and to use limit orders gives you a wide range of opportunities to reduce your transaction costs and/or to implement market-timing strategies. This characteristic can be particularly important during a large one-day decline in the stock market, since ETFs enable you to liquidate your position during the course of the day, when you first see that prices are falling, rather than at the close of trading.

If I want to be able to make money in a bear market or time the market, which is better to have, an index fund or an ETF?

ETFs can be more useful than index funds for timing the market. An investor who practices market timing can employ certain stock market strategies that can't be used with index funds, such as a technique known as selling short. (I explain this in *Ask Suze...About Stocks and Bonds*.) ETFs are exempt from an uptick rule that requires shares to be sold short only at a price higher than the previous sale. Thus ETFs can be shorted on a downtick, which is very important during the major selloffs that characterize bear markets. Short-selling is a very risky strategy, suitable only for sophisticated investors, and won't be of concern to the vast majority of investors.

I have heard about gold ETFs. Can you tell me more about these?

There are currently two gold ETFs—StreetTracks GLD Shares and iShares Comex Gold Trust IAU. Gold ITFs allow investors to buy gold bullion without having to actually hold the metal itself. Each share represents one-tenth of one ounce of gold. In November 2006 each gold ETF had share prices of about $62. Each share is backed by one-tenth of one ounce of physical gold, deposited with a bank. But please be aware that purchasing a gold ETF comes with a higher capital-gains tax than other ETFs. The tax-law legislation that reduced maximum capital gain to 15 percent excluded collectibles, which includes gold, silver, and platinum. So a gold ETF held for more than one year is taxed at a maximum rate of 28 percent.

Are there ETFs that track indexes other than the S&P 500?

Yes, there are many. There are ETFs that track broad indexes of thousands of stocks, such as Vanguard Total Stock Market Index (ticker symbol: VTI). You can invest, for example, in ETFs that track the Standard & Poor's MidCap 400 Depository Receipts (the symbol is MDY), which might appeal to investors seeking more rapid growth than the S&P 500 offers and who are willing to accept greater volatility. If you're looking for more stability, look to invest in a fixed-income ETF that tracks bond indexes such as the iShares Lehman 1–3 year US Treasury Index Bond Fund (symbol SHY). Want to buy an index that tracks 100 technology stocks like Microsoft, Cisco, and Intel? You can do that through the NASDAQ 100 (symbol QQQQ). There are even nine individual Select Sector ETF funds that can give you ownership in a particular sector or groups of industries that are represented by a specified Select Sector Index. The nine Select Sector Indexes on which the Select Sector ETF funds are based together comprise all the companies included in the benchmark S&P 500. As you can see, unit trusts are proliferating. You can pick and choose among them, much as you would among particular stocks, exercising informed judgment on promising sectors and balancing your higher-risk investments with more conservative options. For a list of current ETFs, please go to *http://finance .yahoo.com/etf/browser/mkt?ce-290.*

FUNDS OF FUNDS

There are so many mutual funds out there. Is there a fund that buys other funds?

Yes. This is what is known as a fund of funds (or fofunds). A fofunds is a mutual fund that owns other mutual funds. The great advantage of a fofunds is that you get broad diversification in just one fund. A fund of funds does what you would do by assembling your own portfolio of mutual funds.

Are there disadvantages to funds of funds?

There can be, depending on the fund. You will have to pay the managing and operating fees of not only the fund you purchase but also of each fund within the fund. This can get to be very, very expensive. Also, you don't pick the funds that the fund manager buys, so you'd better like the portfolio manager of the fund you are buying into.

Are there fofunds that do not layer all those commissions?

Funds that buy funds from their own family generally don't layer expenses. TIAA-CREF Managed Allocation TIMAX has no expense ratio, for instance. Nor do funds of funds from The Vanguard Group, or T. Rowe Price. Fidelity's Freedom funds' expense ratios range from .51 percent to .79 percent, but their portfolios do evolve over time. The Vanguard Group is always a great family in which to look for funds with low expenses.

Are there any funds of funds that buy multiple iShares or ETFs?

Yes. As of the writing of this book, there are two mutual fund companies, Seligman and Federated, offering targeted retirement funds (funds with a portfolio mix tailored to a specific retirement date) that invest in assets with a variety of underlying ETFs. My mentioning these funds does not mean that I recommend them; I just want you to know that they exist. I expect there will be others for you to choose from soon.

WHAT TO LOOK FOR WHEN PICKING A MUTUAL FUND

How do I decide which mutual fund is right for me?

First of all, you need to know your investment objective. What do you want to accomplish with the money you are about to invest? Do you want growth over five years, ten years, or longer? Do you want income starting now? A combination of both? After you've figured that out, you should be able to identify dozens of funds that fit your objectives, especially by using a good fund screener, such as the one at *Morningstar .com*. Make up a preliminary list. Then you need to examine the nuts and bolts of each of the funds and compare performance, expense ratios, turnover ratios, sales charges, and policies on cash reserves. Two good sources of general and specific information are SmartMoney.com *(www.smartmoney.com)* and Morningstar *(www.morningstar.com)*.

What is an expense ratio?

Mutual funds have all sorts of ongoing annual expenses that they charge the funds' investors. These include a management fee, as well as operating costs. Together, all these fees add up to what's called the *expense ratio* of the fund. Whatever the expense ratio is, it will definitely affect your rate of return.

I would never buy a fund with an expense ratio higher than 1 percent. Here's why: Let's say that during the course of one year, your mutual fund makes a return of 10 percent. Do you get that 10 percent? Of course not. Before you get your money, the fund subtracts the expense ratio. If the expense ratio is 2 percent, your return will be 7.25 percent. Calculate the effect this high expense ratio has on the growth of your money over time, and you will be amazed.

One of my favorite index funds, Vanguard Total Stock Market Fund, has a total expense ratio of 0.20 percent, and it does really well. Why in the world would you pay someone to manage your money if that person couldn't consistently outperform the index that his or her fund is comparing its performance to? You wouldn't.

What is the turnover rate?

The turnover rate of a mutual fund refers to the cumulative dollar amount of securities that the fund manager buys or sells in a given year. A mutual fund with a 100 percent turnover rate has "turned over" the entire dollar amount of its portfolio.

What is the significance of a 100 percent turnover rate?

The higher the turnover rate, the more likely it is that you have a very aggressive fund manager; the lower the rate, the more conservative the manager. Personally, I prefer portfolio turnover rates of 20 percent to 50 percent—especially if the money is outside of a retirement account. This is because the higher the turnover rate, the more capital-gains taxes you may have to pay at year's end, and the more commissions the fund has to pay to cover all the trades.

Is a 300 percent turnover rate a bad sign, then?

No, not necessarily. But I still would feel better about a lower turnover rate—not more than 50 percent. Again, a portfolio with a high turnover rate may generate lots of year-end taxes, and if your mutual fund is not part of a retirement account, this could mean tax trouble.

Do index funds have a turnover rate?
Yes, but usually only about 5 percent per year. This is because the portfolio manager does not buy and sell stocks based on an active investment strategy. He does so only to match the index he is tracking.

What is the cash reserve of a fund?
A fund's cash reserve is the amount of actual cash kept by a fund to buy stocks or bonds. A fund's cash reserve is an indicator of how the portfolio manager feels about the overall stock market. If there's a large cash reserve, the fund is not fully invested, probably because its manager fears the market will go down and he or she doesn't want to risk exposure or wants to have available cash to buy stocks at a reduced price. On the other hand, if the cash reserve is low, then the fund is more fully invested, suggesting that the fund's manager feels confident that the market is the best place to realize high returns.

In a bull market, I like funds that need to be totally, completely invested all the time, as index funds are. If a mutual fund keeps a large percentage of its money in cash during a period of rising stock prices, then the overall return will most likely not be as high.

What is the "beta" of a mutual fund?
There are several ways to determine your mutual fund's volatility—how much the share price, or NAV, goes up and down

within any given period of time. One is to look at the fund's "beta"—a measure of the volatility of your mutual fund in comparison to the overall market. A mutual fund with a beta of 1 is projected to move in direct correlation to the stock market. If the market goes up 10 percent, the share price, or NAV, of this fund should also move up 10 percent. If the mutual fund you are considering has a beta greater than 1, then the fund will probably move faster—both up and down— than the overall market. The higher the beta, the more aggressive, and therefore riskier, the fund.

What if my mutual fund has a beta of less than 1?

Your mutual fund has been *less* volatile than the market. In downtimes, it may not dip as low as the market, but in boon times, it probably won't match sharp market gains, either.

Are moving averages a reliable way to make decisions about investing?

Moving averages are useful, but a moving average should be only a part of the decision to buy or sell shares of a mutual fund.

Should I buy a fund based on its past performance?

A fund's performance history can't predict what will happen after you buy the fund. A fund's great performance may be the temporary result of special circumstances like investing in a hot sector—think of Internet stocks in the late 90s—and not from impressive overall strategy and management. On the other hand, a fund's past performance provides useful information— specifically, whether the fund is stable or not. Has it stayed in line with what the market did? Or did it wander? Has its share price, or NAV, increased steadily over three, five, and ten years?

If you are buying a managed mutual fund, in particular, look for a stable fund that outperforms the most comparable market index.

What is the yield of a fund? How is it determined?

The yield is what a fund pays to investors in dividends over the course of a year, either in cash payments or by reinvesting in additional shares of the mutual fund. Yield is the ratio of dividends to the NAV. So, for example, if the NAV of your mutual fund is $12, and your mutual fund pays $0.72 a year in dividends, then the yield is 6 percent ($0.72 ÷ $12).

What does the total return of a fund tell me?

The total return is a measure of all realized and unrealized appreciation or depreciation of the fund's investments for a stated period, plus any dividends the fund pays. The total return is a particularly salient statistic when it comes to bond funds. In a bond fund, you can get a yield of 5 or 6 percent, but, at the same time, the NAV of the bond fund may have declined. The total return of the fund, then, taking into consideration the yield and the decline of the NAV, could be a negative figure. Total return is the only figure that counts when analyzing a mutual fund's performance.

How much money can I expect to make in a mutual fund?

Historically, mutual funds that buy and sell common stocks have a return of about 10 percent annually. But keep in mind that this figure is a historical average. You could lose 15 percent one year and make 25 percent the next—which means your average yearly return would be 3.125 percent (because you'll earn the 25 percent on a smaller amount after you've lost 15 percent). However, over time and with patience, you should make money.

EVALUATING RISK

I'm ready to buy a mutual fund, I think. Would you caution me against anything in particular?
Yes—impatience. Remember that mutual funds are long-term investments. It takes time and effort to find the right one. Don't chase after the flavor-of-the-moment fund or the fund that somebody in a chat room gave you a tip about. Don't invest to make a quick killing either, because more often than not, you'll be disappointed.

Are you telling me not to take any risks?
No. Much of the *emotional* benefit of managing your money responsibly comes from discovering how you feel about risk—and learning to accommodate and respect what you discover. If you are an inexperienced investor, I would advise against taking great risks. But I would also advise against playing it too safe—say, with all your money in a money-market account or CDs. And all investors should guard against potential losses on higher-risk investments by balancing them with low-risk investments. Consider investing in two or three mutual funds. That way, if one of your funds outperforms the market and another underperforms or even loses value, you stand a good chance of coming out even, if not ahead, and you'll learn what works for you.

I'm young—can't I afford to take risks?

Yes, you can afford to take more risk because, statistically, the risk evens out with time, and time is on your side. For young investors, as well as those who are unmarried and childless, I would recommend investing some portion of your investment dollars in aggressive growth funds. The older you are and the more financial responsibilities you assume, the more I recommend that you concentrate on balancing your growth (which can be risky) with keeping your capital safe and sound in a mixture of growth funds, balanced funds, and income funds.

RATING MUTUAL FUNDS

When I read financial magazines, they each name a different mutual fund as the best of the year. How is that possible?

Good question. It is strange, isn't it? The answer is that each magazine uses a different formula and factors to calculate the funds' returns. They compare funds to different indexes, and they each have their own methods of analyzing the risks that the funds take.

What factors should I use to rank the mutual funds I'm interested in?

Again, consider a fund's three-, five-, and ten-year performance history. Find out whether the fund has had the same manager for the last few years. But remember, just because a fund's manager did well in the past is not a guarantee that he or his fund will continue to perform well.

I would also go over the following checklist for every fund you consider.

- How has the fund performed compared to other funds that invest similarly? Not all funds, even though they may be the same *kind* of fund, are alike.
- How risky is the fund? If the fund has had a great performance but the risk it had to take to get it was extremely high, then this fund may not be right for you.
- How efficient is the fund? Get the prospectus and annual report of every mutual fund that interests you, and compare the funds' management, expenses, loads, fees, charges, distributions, tax implications, and services.
- How do professionals rank the fund? Use online services that rank the funds for you. The rating service Morningstar *(www.morningstar.com)* is my favorite.

I am afraid that the market may go down after I invest in it, and I'll lose a lot of money. What can I do to limit my exposure?

You can use a technique I love—dollar cost averaging. Please see *Ask Suze . . . About Stocks and Bonds* for complete instructions.

I still don't feel that I have what it takes to pick my funds myself. Is there an unbiased resource that can help me?

One of my favorite resources is a newsletter called the *Bob Brinker Marketimer* (to order, call (914) 591-2655). Brinker is also on ABC radio for three hours every Saturday and Sunday. He's had his show for more than a decade and gives terrific advice on which funds to buy and sell. Brinker also has a website: *www.bobbrinker.com.*

How to Buy a Mutual Fund

When I'm ready to buy a mutual fund, should I contact the company?

Yes, if only to talk to customer service and request a prospectus.

What is a prospectus?

A prospectus is a legal document that describes, usually in some detail, a mutual fund's investment goals, performance, and expenses. It also tells you who manages the fund. Anyone can request a prospectus; in fact, federal law requires that you receive a prospectus when you invest in any mutual fund.

If you're unsure of a fund's name but are interested in, say, aggressive growth funds, a fund company will be able to send you information on various funds that meet your investment objectives.

What exactly is included in a prospectus?

A mutual fund's prospectus includes an explanation of the objectives of the fund. It has tables that compare the fund's performance over the past several years with that of various indexes, such as the S&P 500; a brief analysis of the risks of investing in the fund; and a schedule of any fees that may be charged to investors. You can find out from the prospectus whether the mutual fund is a growth or an income fund. The prospectus will also tell you who manages the fund. Typically, you will not find a current listing of the securities that the mutual fund owns, mostly because they may change from one month to the next.

I've got my prospectus in hand, and it's pretty intimidating.

Look for the important facts: the sales charges, the objective of the fund, the fees and expenses, and the manager. Then, if you haven't already done so, use your rating tools to compare it to other funds with similar objectives.

The prospectus in front of me says that the mutual fund is interested in "capital appreciation." What kind of mutual fund is this?

It's a growth fund. "Capital appreciation" means growth.

A section in the prospectus explains the fund's fees. What should I be on the lookout for?

When you examine the fund's management fees, you want to see no more than 0.25 percent to 1 percent for annual fund expenses. You will also find a list of fees for services—things such as electronic transfers. Also, check to see if the fund charges you for reinvesting dividends. And read the fine print for other minor operational expenses. But, most important, you want to see if the fund is a load fund or a no-load fund.

Basically, load funds cost you money to buy or sell, and no-load funds are free. In my opinion, no-load funds are the way to go. The next section explains why.

SALES CHARGES

Over the years, mutual funds have become immensely popular, so it is important to understand how they really work. When mutual funds first came on the scene, you could buy them only through a broker or financial adviser. They were all what is known as "loaded funds," which means that there's a sales charge on the initial purchase and on every subsequent transaction. Then, slowly but surely, a new breed of mutual funds emerged—"no-load" funds, which do not charge commissions. Investors soon recognized the value of no-load funds and started investing heavily in them. This put a big dent in the profits of brokerage firms that sold only loaded funds, so they came up with another kind of fund—in my opinion, a way to make you think you can buy a no-load fund when you're not buying one. Thus was born the back-end-load fund.

The three most common types of sales charges for mutual funds are front-end-load funds, no-load funds, and back-end-load funds. The load funds charge you a commission fee up front for buying the fund. No-load funds carry no commission fee, although, like all funds, they have some maintenance fees. With back-end-load funds, you may pay when you take your money out of the fund.

What are front-end-load funds?
Front-end-load funds are identified as A-share mutual funds. If the name of a mutual fund contains "A" or "A shares," it's a front-end-load fund. Front-end-load funds charge a fee, or a load, up front. This is the commission that the broker or the

financial planner takes before your money gets invested. The commission can be anywhere from 2 percent to 8.5 percent; the average commission is about 5 percent—out of your pocket! Think of this load as an unnecessary tax on your money.

What are no-load funds?

No-load funds are mutual funds that don't cost you a penny to buy or to sell. In other words, they don't have a load (commission). I believe no-load mutual funds are the only kind to buy. Look at it this way: If you were to invest $10,000 in a no-load mutual fund and you decided, two days later, that you wanted to withdraw your money, you'd get all $10,000 back, assuming the market hadn't moved. If you invested $10,000 in a loaded fund and wanted your money back, you would get back only about $9,500. Think about that—a loaded fund has to go up approximately 5 percent for you just to break even. That means you are starting out with a 5 percent disadvantage in a loaded fund.

What are back-end-load funds, also known as 12(b)1 funds or B shares?

In my opinion, B shares are the worst kind. B shares are back-end-loaded shares that lock you in to a period of time—usually five to seven years—during which you cannot sell the fund without being hit with a "surrender" charge, or load. This load usually starts at 5 percent if you sell during the first year, and drops to 4 percent the second, 3 percent the third, 2 percent the fourth, and 1 percent the fifth. You pay nothing if you sell thereafter.

My broker told me a back-end-load fund wouldn't cost me anything if I just stayed in it for ten years. What's so bad about that?

I can't tell you how angry this makes me. What your broker failed to tell you is that you *are* paying to be in that fund. You see, the broker who sold you the fund probably received a 5 percent commission, paid by either the firm he works for or the fund itself, up front and in full when you made the purchase. The brokerage firm or mutual fund company gets its money back by charging you what is known as a 12(b)1 fee of anywhere from 0.25 to 1 percent yearly, which is included in the expense ratio. This fee, which the SEC allows for "marketing" costs, is used to pay the cost of the broker and is taken out of the fund's returns. So if your fund earns 10 percent, and your 12(b)1 fee is 1 percent, your return is only 9 percent, because the brokerage firm is taking that 1 percent to pay itself back for the broker's commission. That is why your surrender fee goes down by 1 percent each year. Suppose your fund paid a broker 5 percent up front and they take 1 percent a year from your return. If you were to sell after one year, your surrender charge would be 4 percent. Add that to the 1 percent they already took, and they've recouped the money they paid the broker. Pretty sneaky, don't you think?

Some B shares automatically convert to A shares after the surrender period, but some do not, and you continue to pay that 12(b)1 fee every year for as long as you own the fund—even though the broker has already been paid! Again, in my opinion, B shares came about simply because brokerage firms needed to find a way to keep your business by luring you into a load fund in the guise of a no-load fund.

Can you illustrate the effect of 12(b)1 fees?
I sure can. On the following page are the actual returns of a growth fund from a major brokerage firm that has both A and B shares. Note the difference between the returns of the two. Remember that these are shares of the *same fund,* managed by

COMPARISON OF A- AND B-SHARE RETURNS OVER TIME

ANNUAL RETURN PERCENTAGE	FIRST YEAR	SECOND YEAR
A Shares	28.70	33.49
B Shares	27.19	32.05
Difference	1.51	1.44

TRAILING RETURN PERCENTAGE	ONE-YEAR AVERAGE	THREE-YEAR AVERAGE
A Shares	19.88	27.86
B Shares	18.54	26.45
Difference	1.34	1.41

the same portfolio manager. The only difference is that one set of returns is on the A shares and the other is on the B shares.

Take a good look and you will see the return on the A shares is more than 1 percentage point higher than the return on the B shares. Why? Because of that 12(b)1 fee that you are paying out of your own pocket! If you look at the trailing return percentage, which is your average return if your money was in the mutual fund for all of one or three years, you will see that the 12(b)1 fee again makes more than a percent difference in your return. And this is the same fund with the same holdings and the same manager. But B shareholders realize a lower return—because they are paying the fund out of their return!

Is the 12(b)1 charge in lieu of any other charges in my mutual fund?

Hardly. The 12(b)1 fee is in *addition* to all the other fees. You still have to pay the management fees and other expenses of the fund, just as you do with a no-load fund or an A-share fund. The 12(b)1 fees exist only to pay the broker's or financial adviser's commission.

Why would my financial adviser try to sell me these B shares of a fund?

Because that's how he makes a living. Choose your financial adviser carefully—good financial advice informs you, the client, how to get the most from your money, even if it means the adviser won't make a lot of money from the transaction. Advisers are there to help you get rich, not to get rich off you. It's the adviser's responsibility to tell you if there's a less expensive way for you to make money—and to give you the choice of what you want to do.

Does a loaded fund perform better than a no-load fund?

The sales commission has absolutely nothing to do with the performance of a mutual fund; performance is based on the performance of an index (for index funds) and the talent of a manager (for managed funds). From that performance, you can deduct expenses—including sales commissions—so in fact for a load fund to outperform, it much overcome it expenses.

So what you're saying is that if I am going to use a financial adviser to buy a fund, I'm better off buying A shares than B shares?

Yes. If, for whatever reason, you still want to use a financial adviser to buy a loaded mutual fund, you are better off buying A shares than B shares. If you do buy A shares, make sure you ask your broker about the breakpoint for the load on the fund you are thinking about buying.

What is a breakpoint?

The breakpoint is the amount of money you have to invest in a fund in order to pay a reduced commission. The amount varies from fund to fund but, in general, the more money you invest, the lower the sales load will be. The first breakpoint level for many mutual funds is $25,000. Keep in mind that breakpoints apply only to loaded mutual funds. In a no-load fund, obviously, there's no load that you need a break from.

I have heard that investors can qualify for a breakpoint if they sign a letter of intent. What is this?

A letter of intent (LOI) tells the mutual fund that eventually you will invest an amount of money equal to one of the fund's breakpoint levels. (It's not uncommon for mutual funds to have more than one breakpoint level.) If you write a letter of intent, then you will not be charged the higher sales load.

How long do I have before I must actually invest this money?

Typically, you have 13 months.

What if 13 months passes and I haven't invested the entire amount?

An LOI isn't legally binding. However, if you have not reached the investment level you stipulated in the LOI, you will be penalized by the fund for the difference between the lower load that you paid and the regular sales commission.

What is a right of accumulation?

For the investor who doesn't qualify for a breakpoint, a right of accumulation provides a lower commission if the investor manages to reach a certain investment threshold over several years' time. Although the lower load is not retroactive, the new, reduced load applies to all future purchases, as well as to the purchase that catapulted the investor over the breakpoint limit.

What is a redemption fee?

A redemption fee is a percentage the fund charges you to withdraw your money from that fund. This is different from a back load or a surrender fee, which usually goes away after a period of time. A redemption fee is in place for the life of the fund, and it usually runs about 1.5 percent. It is important that you know whether or not your fund has a redemption fee.

Do no-load funds have redemption fees?

It's not very common, but some no-load funds have them.

My broker tells me that all mutual funds have loads. Is this true?

Well, it is true that all mutual funds have expense ratios, and some are higher than others. This expense ratio, a percentage of the total investment in the fund, pays the salary of the portfolio manager who is buying and selling the stocks and/or bonds, as well as expenses incurred in actually running the fund.

However, the actual sales load, or broker commission, which is what we are referring to here, is an entirely separate issue. Not all funds have sales loads, and those that do, in my opinion, are a waste of your money.

So are you telling me that a no-load mutual fund is the only way to go?

That is exactly what I am saying. There are some 2,500 mutual funds out there that charge no commission whatsoever to invest with them. What's more, no-load funds can be purchased without the help of an adviser—no middleman, no commissions, no hidden costs, just smooth sailing to what might be greater and greater wealth over time.

How can I find a listing of all the no-load funds that are out there?

Once again, I prefer the website *Morningstar.com*. It has one of the most complete sets of listings anywhere—although even this excellent site may not list every single one of the hundreds of no-load funds in existence. After you log on, choose Morningstar's Mutual Fund Screener, in the Funds section, then select No-Load Funds. You can refine your search in any way you choose.

Can I save money by investing in mutual funds online?

Not if you are buying a no-load fund. A no-load fund will not cost you anything if you buy it directly through the company, so, in this case, trading or purchasing online will not save you money—in fact, it may add a fee.

I want to buy a no-load fund from a discount brokerage firm, but it charges a fee. Is this a load?

No. This is known as a *transaction fee*. If you don't want to pay it, just buy the fund directly through the fund family itself. And there are discount brokers who don't charge a transaction fee. It's worth your while to check around.

WHEN TO BUY AND WHEN TO SELL

A mutual fund is a long-term investment, so before you buy one, be sure to track its progress for a few months. What exactly should you be looking for? Look for answers to the following four questions: How rapidly has your fund been growing or shrinking in size—that is, attracting or losing assets? How risky has your fund been? How has your fund performed in relation to other, similar funds? And how long has your fund had the same manager? Once you've bought your mutual fund, keep asking these questions; when the answers are no longer satisfactory to you, you'll know that it's time to consider selling.

How do I decide whether to buy or sell a mutual fund?
The decision to buy or sell a mutual fund should begin with performance, and the best way to evaluate the performance of any mutual fund is to compare it to an appropriate benchmark. A fund that consistently performs below its benchmark is a strong candidate for sale.

BENCHMARKS

What is a benchmark?
Benchmarks—or something to measure your fund's performance against—come in many different varieties, but an index or index mutual fund is the preferred benchmark for most

professional money managers. For example, the Standard & Poor's 500 stock index or the Vanguard 500 Index mutual fund can be a good benchmark for evaluating the performance of a mutual fund that invests in large-cap U.S. stocks.

How should I use a benchmark to evaluate funds I own or am considering buying?

You will probably want to use a benchmark whose composition is reasonably close to that of the fund you are evaluating. For example, if you are investing in a growth fund, you'll want to measure your fund against a benchmark for growth; if your fund is a large-cap fund, you'll want to compare it with a large-cap index. I'll list some good benchmarks for use with different kinds of funds in the next question. Morningstar's free fund data compares a fund's performance to a relative benchmark, as well as to its category peers.

As a general rule, I suggest that you avoid performance comparisons over very short or very long periods (for example, one month or ten years). I would suggest that you compare the performance of a mutual fund to its benchmark for the past three years. Even better, I think, is to compare a fund's performance to its benchmark over several periods—ideally 12 months, 36 months (three years), and 60 months (five years).

How do I choose a good benchmark fund?

In addition to the index itself, the following mutual funds offer good comparison.

- If you have a *balanced fund,* Vanguard Balanced Index Fund (symbol VBINX) is a good benchmark to use. This is a mutual fund that invests about 60 percent of its assets in large stocks and about 40 percent in high-quality bonds. The stock portfolio attempts to match the performance and risk characteristics of the MSCI US Broad Market Index. The bond portfolio attempts to match the performance and risk characteristics of the Lehman Aggregate Bond Index.

- If you have a *large-cap fund,* try using Vanguard 500 Index Fund (symbol VFINX), a mutual fund that attempts to match the performance and risk characteristics of Standard & Poor's 500 Stock Index.

- If you have a *domestic mid-cap fund,* a good benchmark might be Dreyfus MidCap Index Fund (symbol PESPX), a mutual fund that seeks to match the performance of the Standard & Poor's Mid-Cap 400 Index.

- If you have a *small-cap fund,* you can compare your fund to Vanguard Small-Cap Index Fund (symbol NAESX), a mutual fund that seeks to match the performance and risk characteristics of the MSCI US Small-Cap 1750 Index.

- If you have an *international fund,* you can use Schwab International Index Fund (symbol SWINX), a mutual fund that seeks broad international equity diversification.

DECIDING TO SELL A FUND

Benchmarking is an excellent way to measure the performance of a mutual fund relative to its peers and is a pivotal first step in the process of deciding to sell a mutual fund you own. Before you sell, however, there are a few other things to consider.

What if my mutual fund didn't outperform the S&P 500? Is that a sign that I should get rid of it?

No, not necessarily. In fact, in recent years it's been surprisingly difficult for a managed fund to outperform an index. And even index funds will show lower returns than the index they track, simply because some fees must be deducted. Often, a better way to measure the performance of your mutual fund is by watching the benchmark funds that are most relevant to it.

How does the riskiness of a fund enter into the decision to sell it?

If you want to start a lively discussion among financial professionals, ask each of them to say a few words about "risk" in relation to a mutual fund.

Cutting through the debate, I think that most investors perceive mutual fund risk as the chance of having a "down" year, as well as the magnitude of the potential slide. But mutual fund risk must be viewed in context. For example, imagine that you own Fund A and you are comparing it to a benchmark index fund (Fund B). Fund A is considered to be slightly more aggressive, and slightly riskier, than Fund B. However, Fund A has historically outperformed Fund B, so you might want to keep Fund A, even if there is a good chance that next year it will have a worse year than Fund B. Now let's assume that Fund A has historically performed worse than Fund B. If it is likely that Fund A is going to have a worse year than Fund B, would you continue to hold Fund A? Probably not. In both cases, Fund A is "riskier" than Fund B, but in the first case the greater risk of Fund A has often been rewarded with greater return. In the second case, both risk and return are working against Fund A, and Fund A is a compelling candidate for sale.

What other factors enter into the decision to sell a mutual fund?

The two most important factors to consider are *manager turnover* and *change in fund assets*.

Why is manager turnover important?

By itself, a change in portfolio managers is not a reason to sell a mutual fund. But it is valuable information when you want to evaluate a fund's performance. A change in fund management can explain a pattern of deteriorating performance and reinforce a decision to sell that is based on performance information. In other cases, a recent change in fund management may encourage you to hold on to a fund that has performed poorly.

If your fund has underperformed its benchmark for the past twelve months/three years/five years, and the tenure of your fund manager is five years or greater, you know that the current manager is responsible for the poor performance. This is a strong signal to sell your fund—you've given a manager five years to beat the benchmark, and that manager has failed to do the job.

Now, say your fund has performed poorly for the past twelve months/three years/five years, but the manager is relatively new. Clearly, you can't hold the current manager entirely accountable for the fund's poor performance, but that doesn't mean you should continue to hold on to the fund. If the new fund manager had a good record at a similar fund, you might want to hold. If the new manager has never managed a fund before or has a relatively poor record managing another fund, you should probably sell.

How do you find out about a fund manager's history?

You can usually get that information directly from your fund.

Call the 800 number and request the manager's professional biography.

Will the performance information for the fund always tell me how well the manager is doing?

It isn't easy to correlate performance information to a fund manager. Cause and effect are often hidden. For example, consider a large-cap fund with a manager who has been in charge for two years. The fund has the following performance information relative to the Vanguard 500 Index:

5 Years	-4.5
3 Years	-3.0
12 Months	2.0

In this case, it's reasonable to credit the recent good year to the new manager and to attribute the poor longer-term performance to the previous manager. But is 12 months enough time to form a valid opinion of the new manager? Probably not. The new manager might not have changed the fund's holdings, but the strategy that's been in place just happened to finally work. You might continue to hold this fund, keeping a close eye on the new manager's performance.

Why should I be concerned about a change in the assets of my mutual fund?

Some mutual fund managers are better at managing relatively small sums of money, and their performance may suffer as their asset base grows. Though it may sound counterintuitive, rapid growth of assets under management can help explain a mutual fund's poor recent performance.

For example, consider ABC Small-Cap Fund, a hypothetical

fund that grew from $50 million to $1 billion of assets under management. Let's assume that, at any given time, the manager of ABC Fund has 50 good investment ideas—in other words, a maximum of 50 stocks on his A list. When ABC Fund had $50 million in assets, the fund manager could take an average position of $1 million in each of the 50 stocks on his A list. Now that the fund has to invest $1 billion, the average position must grow to $20 million. The ABC Fund manager is faced with several choices, none of them particularly desirable from the standpoint of the fund's shareholders:

- The portfolio manager can take $20 million (or larger) positions in several of his best choices. However, since many small companies have total market capitalization of only $200 million or so, ABC Fund would probably end up owning 10 percent or more of the stock in several companies. Large positions like this prevent a fund from being liquid. There are also legal restrictions on how concentrated a mutual fund may become in any given company.
- The ABC Fund manager can expand his stock list beyond 50, considering less attractive investment opportunities—moving, in effect, to his B list.
- The manager can raise the median capitalization of his holdings—that is, buy the securities of larger companies—even though he is really only expert in selecting small-cap stocks.

No matter what the ABC manager does, fund performance is likely to suffer.

How will a change in assets affect my decision to sell my mutual fund?

When evaluating information on a change in assets, keep your fund's market capitalization objectives in mind. Generally, small-cap and specialty funds have the hardest time handling large increases or decreases in assets. Large-cap funds can handle asset swings of 10 percent, 20 percent, or more (though this doesn't happen very often). If you own a small-cap or specialty fund with a changing asset base *and* deteriorating performance, you should be concerned. For more information, see the website *fundalarm.com*.

WHEN THINGS CHANGE

Three years ago, I bought a mutual fund that started off great. Lately, it's in a slump. What's going on?

Your mutual fund could be disappointing you for a number of reasons.

If you invested in a growth fund, the market may be in a cycle where the securities typically chosen for growth are temporarily out of favor.

Your fund manager may have made decisions or judgments based on speculation that never paid off. (Remember, it is terribly difficult, if not impossible, to outwit the market.) Your manager might have bet that the stock market was poised for a fall and put a lot of the fund's assets in cash (a hedge against a massive drop in stock prices), but instead the market, against all odds, kept going up.

Your fund could be doing poorly because of instability at home or abroad. Is there a war going on, or the threat of war in the wind? How are the foreign markets doing? Closer to home, what are interest rates doing? What is the unemployment rate? Did your fund manager buy small-cap stocks that may not have moved? There are many reasons a fund does not perform.

My mutual fund just merged with another fund. This fund has a track record that is iffy at best. Should I get out now, before it's too late?
This is a good question. The decision to sell a mutual fund is not based entirely on market performance or financial indicators. If, for any reason, you feel uncomfortable with the fund—for example, your investment objectives have changed, or you're skeptical about the fund's direction—then by all means sell it (as long as you have considered the tax ramifications, of course).

Why would my investment objectives change?
Investors' financial objectives change regularly. The classic example is when investors retire and begin to want more income from their funds. Unexpected events can change your objectives, too. For example, what if you or your spouse were to suddenly fall ill? With the threat of ballooning medical expenses, you might not want your money in a growth-oriented mutual fund. Suddenly, a money-market fund might suit you better.

As you get older, you should reexamine your investment objectives from time to time. If your fund's objectives are no longer in sync with yours, it is time to sell your fund.

Is there a relationship between the strength of the economy and the performance of a mutual fund?
The answer is usually yes, but it depends on what kind of mutual fund you're talking about. Let's use sector funds as an

example. With a sector fund, you are investing in a particular industry—such as chemicals, pharmaceuticals, or medical supplies. What happens when the economy starts to take off? The securities of industries involved in manufacturing, such as heavy metals and chemicals, tend to swing upward, anticipating work and demand. What happens when the economy starts to slow down? The general emphasis of buyers is on slower and steadier industries, such as health care and consumer goods.

What economic signs are important in determining the market's long-term movement, which obviously will affect growth mutual funds?

The financial signs that have the biggest impact on the stock market in general are the following:

- Economic growth
- Interest rates
- Inflation
- Strength of the dollar

What am I looking for as I watch these different indicators?

Well, the stock market is like a pot of soup. For good results, all the ingredients have to be just so. In my opinion, for a truly strong market you need:

- Slow economic growth
- Low interest rates
- Reduced inflationary expectations
- A strong dollar overseas

Are all four factors equally important?

Yes, because they all work off one another. If you have a weak dollar abroad, interest rates tend to rise here in the United States. However, with rising interest rates comes fear of inflation, the stock market's biggest enemy. Understanding how the economy works will help you make informed decisions about whether and when you should sell, buy, or just shift the balance of what you already have.

Is there a good time to buy and sell growth funds?

Whether we're talking about mutual funds or stocks, it's always easier to know when to buy than when to sell. Knowing when to sell is the hardest thing to master. The following guidelines are not set in stone, but they might help you decide.

A good time to buy:

- You won't need the money for at least ten years.
- Your research indicates the fund's assets are undervalued.
- You are looking for diversification and professional management in your investments.

A bad time to buy:

- You need your money within two years.
- You want to keep your money 100 percent safe and sound.
- The fund is about to distribute capital gains to shareholders *and* it's unlikely that the fund's value will increase more than the net tax amount of that distribution. (This only applies to funds outside of retirement accounts.)

A good time to sell:

- There has been a fundamental change in the fund's investment style, which affects your portfolio strategy.
- Your fund has underperformed its competitors for the past couple of years.
- An important portfolio manager leaves.

A bad time to sell:

- Your mutual fund has a big back-end load (or deferred sales charge), and you haven't given the fund a chance to perform.

TAXES, TAXES, TAXES

The following applies only to mutual funds held outside of retirement accounts.

With mutual funds, what will I owe taxes on?

When you sell any shares of your mutual fund held outside a retirement account, you will have to pay taxes on whatever profit you make. If your mutual fund itself makes a profit, meaning the *fund* sells shares of stock at a gain, you will also have to pay capital-gains taxes on that profit, even though you didn't sell any of your shares in the fund. (This is known as a capital-gains distribution.) In either case, the amount of taxes will be different, depending on whether the profits from your mutual fund are considered short-term or long-term (see the next question). You also will owe taxes on dividends that the fund distributes to you or reinvests for you. (You do not have to pay any taxes on income that you earned from tax-free money funds or tax-free municipal bond funds.)

What is the difference between short-term and long-term profits?

Short-term profits are net profits from the sale of a stock or mutual fund that was held 12 months or less. Long-term profits are net profits from the sale of a stock or mutual fund that was held for longer than 12 months. If you have made long-term profits, the most you will be taxed is 15 percent. This rate is set to revert to 20 percent in 2011. Short-term profits are taxed at your ordinary income-tax rate, whatever that may be (currently up to 35 percent, but the current individual tax rates are also set to expire in 2011).

What is a capital-gains distribution?

At the end of every year, all mutual funds that have made gains distribute that money among their investors, who can take the cash or reinvest it in the fund. In both cases, this is an end-of-the-year capital-gains distribution, and it will be taxed.

Why does a fund have to make an end-of-the-year capital-gains distribution?

Mutual funds are not allowed to keep the profits made from the sale of stocks that they own. All profits must be distributed among shareholders.

Am I entitled to this distribution even if I just bought into the fund?

Yes, but this is not necessarily a benefit. You get money, but you also must pay taxes on it. In addition, the fund lowers the price of its shares (or NAV) by the amount of the distribution. Unfortunately, between taxes and a lower share price, an end-of-the-year distribution could end up costing you money.

I still don't understand why such an end-of-the-year gain would be bad.

Let's say that you just bought into a mutual fund at $45 a share at the beginning of December. The NAV of the fund has stayed at about $45 for the whole month. At the end of December, the fund pays out $3 per share in short-term capital-gains distributions. To reflect this distribution, the fund lowers the price of the shares to $42. You now will owe taxes on that $3. Let's say you are in the 30 percent combined federal and state tax bracket. You will now owe $0.90 of that $3 to the government in taxes. That leaves you with $2.10. Add that to the price of the mutual fund, and you now have a total of $44.10. Of course, you bought the shares at $45 apiece. Because of the capital-gains distribution, you now have a paper loss of $0.90 a share. Worse, if you owned a lot of shares of that mutual-fund company, the distribution of short-term gains could be large enough to bump you into a higher tax bracket, costing you even more money.

If I reinvest my capital-gains distribution, do I still have to pay taxes on it?

If you're investing outside of a retirement account, yes. Taxes are always owed, regardless of whether you keep or reinvest your end-of-the-year distribution.

So is the lesson to avoid investing in a mutual fund in the month of December?

Not necessarily. If the fund went up in value between the time you bought it and the year's end—and it went up by more than the amount of the taxes you will owe on the capital-gains distribution—you would benefit. For example, let's say that a fund is going to hand out 5 percent in capital-gains distributions at the end of the year. You will have to pay tax on that 5 percent distribution. Assuming that you are in a 30 percent tax bracket, 1.5 percent of that gain will be lost to taxes. So your decision comes down to this: Do you think the fund will appreciate by more than 1.5 percent before the end of the year? How clear is your crystal ball?

It's impossible to say that it's *always* better to wait until the beginning of the next year to invest simply to avoid capital-gains taxes. Sometimes it is, and sometimes it isn't.

Please remember two things: First, end-of-the-year capital gains are a potential problem only if you own funds outside of a retirement account. In a retirement account, capital-gains distributions do not matter, since you do not pay taxes currently on that money anyway. Second, not every mutual fund makes significant capital-gains distributions.

Are there funds that don't make capital-gains distributions?

Yes. Index funds, for example. Since index funds buy all the companies in a given index, they do not generally distribute large capital gains. Why? Because they need to buy and sell only when one of the stocks of the index is removed and replaced. This happens rarely, so trades occur with nothing like the frequency they do in a managed fund. If the thought of paying taxes on unexpected capital gains worries you, buy into an index fund. There are also mutual funds that are known as tax-efficient funds. Managers of tax-efficient funds aim to keep a low turnover ratio in their portfolios.

Can I avoid capital-gains distributions with a low-turnover-ratio fund?

Unfortunately, no. If you buy an index fund, turnover ratio will not be a problem. However, even if a fund has a low turnover ratio, that does not mean it won't have a large capital gain one day. By the late 1990s, for example, many managed funds had in their portfolios stocks that they had held for years. Even funds that don't buy and sell stocks at a high frequency have so-called embedded capital gains, which come from long-held stocks. Embedded capital gains are earnings that a fund has in its stock portfolio that it has not yet cashed in or realized.

How do embedded capital gains work?

Here's an example: Suppose Fund A has a low turnover ratio and has owned a certain technology stock for two years. This stock accounts for nearly 20 percent of the fund's portfolio. For one reason or another, the fund manager decides that he now wants to liquidate the entire holding of this stock, which, let's say, is currently trading at $350 a share. The original purchase price of the stock—or its "cost basis"—was $50. With a profit of $300 per share, you can imagine the capital-gains tax you will owe, even at the new reduced rate of 15 percent for long-term gains. If you really want to avoid unexpected capital-gains taxes, ETFs are the way to go.

I received a dividend from my mutual fund this January, but on my statement it said that it was declared in December of the previous year. Do I owe taxes on this money for last year?

You sure do. Often a mutual fund will declare a dividend at the end of the calendar year but not pay it until January of the following year. Nevertheless, you are considered to have received the dividend in the year in which it was declared. The maximum tax you will pay will be only 15 percent. (In 2011, though, the dividend tax rate may rise again, reverting to your ordinary income-tax rate.)

If I sell a mutual fund I have lost money in, can I write off the loss?

Yes—but *only* if you sold the fund and have a realized loss, not just a paper loss. Be advised that there is a maximum deduction for capital losses during a single year—currently $3,000—unless you have capital gains to offset them. If you have gains, you can offset an equal amount of losses against them.

If I sell my mutual fund, how will I know what gains (if any) to report on my income taxes?

Your mutual fund company will send you a Form 1099-DIV, which informs you what you must report on your tax return.

I have read that capital-gains distributions must be added to the original share price of mutual funds. Does this apply if the capital gains were not reinvested in the mutual fund?

No. If the gains were not reinvested, nothing changes in regard to your holdings. However, if you reinvest your gains into the fund, where they are used to buy additional shares of the fund, they become part of your original share price (or cost basis).

I have accumulated a lot of shares in a mutual fund over the last few years, and now I want to start selling

just a few of them off. What is the best way to do that, tax-wise?

I would sell off the shares that have the highest cost basis first. This will lessen your immediate tax burden. However, not many people keep track of the dates that they purchased shares of a mutual fund and what their cost basis, or purchase price, was at the time. Most mutual fund companies provide only an *average cost basis,* which is the average price for all the shares that you have purchased. You can use this figure to calculate your capital-gains taxes.

SYSTEMATIC WITHDRAWAL

I want to stay invested in the stock market, but I need money to live on. Is there a way to get money out of my growth fund on a monthly basis?

Yes. Systematic withdrawal is an ideal option for people who want to leave money in a fund for growth, yet need money to live on. In this arrangement, your mutual fund company redeems a certain amount of your shares every month and sends you the full sale-price amount. The stock market historically has grown at a rate of about 11 percent a year, averaged over time, and most people can afford to take a share of that, say 4 or 5 percent, out of their mutual funds every year without depleting the principal.

What if there's a bear market?

Then you can call your mutual fund company and arrange to take less in your systematic withdrawal. If there's a raging bull market, you can arrange for more. It's your money, and it's up to you.

Will I have to pay taxes on the amount that the mutual fund sends me every month?

It will depend on whether you have realized a gain over your purchase price. If you do, you will. If you don't, you won't.

Does systematic withdrawal work with all types of mutual funds, or just certain kinds?

This is a crucial question, and the answer is that systematic withdrawal works best, naturally, with a high-performing fund. That means either a growth fund, or a growth-and-income fund. Since these funds typically invest in blue-chip stocks, the chances of these funds faltering are significantly lower. I would not use the systematic-withdrawal system to take money out of a bond fund. These funds typically don't grow very quickly, so you may be unintentionally gnawing away at your principal. In fact, regardless of the kind of fund you're in, you may be chipping away at your principal. If you need income and you cannot risk losing any of the principal that is generating this income, then individual bonds would be a far better investment option.

BEWARE OF FALSE DIVERSIFICATION

Over the years, many of you will accumulate a number of mutual funds. And you may believe that you have a nicely diversified portfolio. But this may not be true. Although you own several funds, it is possible that the top ten holdings of each of these funds may be identical stocks. In the 90s many investors had money in five or six growth mutual funds. The top ten holdings in those funds were all almost surely tech stocks, and most likely the same tech stocks: Cisco, Intel, Microsoft, etc. Things were going great in the late 90s, but these investors probably saw their profits and even some of their principal go down the drain in the year 2000. To be truly diversified, it's important that the holdings in your many mutual funds are not all the same.

Where can I look to find out what my mutual funds' holdings are?

Simply go to *www.morningstar.com* or *www.smartmoney.com* and compare the top ten holdings of each of your mutual funds.

Besides the holdings of the stocks within a mutual fund, how else should I be diversified when buying a mutual fund? How many funds should a person own?

If you can invest your money for growth for at least ten years, the ideal scenario is to own ten mutual funds, two in each of the following areas:

Large-growth stocks
Large-value stocks
Small-growth stocks
Small-value stocks

But with today's ETFs and index funds, most of your needs can be covered with just one or two funds. Consider an index fund or ETF that buys the Wilshire 5000 index, as well as a fund that buys an international index.

Is there a website that will compare my mutual funds for me to show me how well I am diversified?

If you go to *www.morningstar.com,* you will really be able to find almost anything and everything that you need to help you evaluate the funds that you currently have.

BASICS OF BOND FUNDS

What is a bond fund?

A bond fund is simply a mutual fund that is made up entirely of bonds. Bond funds come in all shapes and sizes, just as bonds do, but the interest rate on a bond fund is not fixed, as it most often is on a single bond. It will fluctuate along with interest rates in the economy. Bond funds pay income every month, however, and investors like knowing that they can rely on that check. Another difference: Bond funds do not have a maturity date. In other words, there is never a fixed date on which you will get back your principal investment. You have to sell your shares in the bond fund in order to get your money back, and those shares will rise or fall in value according to whether interest rates are rising or falling. In spite of the fact that the fund does not mature, however, the bonds within the fund do mature.

Why does the interest rate for a bond fund fluctuate?

The interest rate moves in tandem with interest rates in the economy, as the rates on individual bonds do, but the fund rate will lag behind them a bit.

What's the significance of the fact that bond funds don't have maturity dates?

Because bond funds don't have maturity dates, you can't be

sure how much of your original investment you will get back when you sell your shares. You might get more than you paid, or less. Let's say that you decide to sell your bond fund shares at a time when interest rates have risen since you originally purchased them. Because your fund has a lower interest rate than newer funds do, your shares won't be in much demand and you will most likely get back less than the full amount you invested in the fund. But the reverse is also true. If interest rates have fallen since your original purchase, you will probably get back more than you invested when you sell your shares. This uncertainty about how much of your original investment you'll be able to recoup is a big difference between bond funds and individual bonds.

What determines whether the price of the bond fund goes up or down?

Primarily, it's the old seesaw of general interest rates that determines whether bond fund shares gain or decrease in value: If interest rates go up, the price of the shares of the bond fund will tend to fall. If they go down, the price of the shares of the bond fund will tend to rise.

Is that price movement guaranteed to be predictable?

No, which is another disadvantage of bond funds. If the fund is poorly managed, the price of the fund could go down and you could lose money even if interest rates fall.

Why would I want to invest in a bond fund?

Bond funds are useful as parking places for your money while you ponder a decision about what else to do with it—before making a big consumer purchase, say, or undertaking a make-over of your investment portfolio. Money-market funds and

CDs (certificates of deposit) are technically bond funds, and are particularly suitable for parking.

KINDS OF BOND FUNDS

Now that you know the different characteristics of bond funds, you need to know the different categories. Remember that each one of these bond funds can be made up of long- or short-term maturities. Categories include U.S. Treasury bond funds, municipal bond funds, mortgage-backed security funds held by U.S. agencies, corporate bond funds, and international bond funds. Let's take a look at them in order.

What is a U.S. Treasury bond fund?
A Treasury bond fund invests exclusively in U.S. Treasury bills, bonds, and notes. Most people who invest in Treasury bond funds are looking for absolute safety in terms of the quality of the bonds in the portfolio. But remember, even with Treasury bonds, the price per share of your fund can fluctuate according to interest-rate movements.

What is a municipal bond fund?
A municipal bond fund invests in various municipal bonds whose interest is paid by cities, counties, and/or states. If you are considering investing in one of these, please check to be sure the fund manager insures the bonds in the fund.

I assume that whether or not a municipal bond fund is insured affects its yield—am I right?
Yes. Insured municipal bond funds have to pay for their insurance, and what they pay comes out of the shareholders' take.

Do all municipal bond funds escape taxation?

Partly, but not wholly. The same tax rules that apply to individual municipal bonds apply here. In order to avoid state taxes, you must buy a municipal bond fund that invests only in bonds from the state in which you are a resident.

How do I know if a municipal bond fund has my state's bonds in it?

The name of the bond fund will include your state's name, as in the Vanguard California Tax-Free Fund.

If my state does not have a state income tax, should I still buy a municipal bond fund that invests only in bonds issued by my state?

No. Buy the municipal bond or bond fund that will give you the highest yield regardless of the state, keeping in mind your tolerance for risk, of course.

What is a mortgage-backed security fund?

Let's take Ginnie Mae bond funds as an example. Investments in individual Ginnie Mae bonds are used to finance home mortgages across the country. Ginnie Mae bond funds are made up of Ginnie Mae bonds. The funds pay a little more than most Treasury bond funds do and, as with individual Ginnie Maes, there is a federal guarantee behind them. However, the funds have some of the same disadvantages as the bonds do. For one thing, your income is derived from monthly mortgage payments, so you have to be on the lookout for declining interest rates; in a period of declining rates, many homeowners decide to refinance, paying off their entire original mortgage at once. This means that your bond fund, which holds those mortgages, will get back a large chunk of its principal sooner than expected. The fund will then transfer that principal to you. This means that you will have to reinvest the principal.

What should I know about corporate bond funds?

Such funds are made up of bonds issued by corporations. By definition, they are less safe than government bond funds, but they pay you a higher yield. In my opinion, however, individual corporate bonds are a better way to go than corporate bond funds.

How can I get the highest yield from a corporate bond fund?

The highest-yielding bond funds are also the riskiest. Many high-yield, or junk, bond funds offer very attractive interest rates, and investors light up like pinball machines when they hear they can get a 2 percent higher yield per year than they could get with most other bond funds. But there are risks—almost as many with the funds as with the individual bonds. If the companies that issue these bonds default, investors in individual bonds may get little or nothing back—no interest and little or no principal. Investing in a high-yield bond fund means you do not risk the loss of all your principal and interest, but if even one company in the fund defaults, it can cause the fund's share price to drop dramatically. Always remember that the longer the average maturity of the bonds in your fund, the higher its yield and the greater the risk. Add junk bonds to this mix, and you will find yourself the owner of a very high-risk, potentially high-yielding bond fund. You can buy funds containing high-yield bonds of almost any kind, including municipal bonds. Most of the issuers are cities or companies that have low credit ratings. Do you really want to take this chance with your money? You might or might not, depending on the interest rate and the specific cities or companies involved.

Last, what about international bond funds?

These are funds that invest in bonds of foreign countries, but please note that they are not for the first-time bond fund investor. The least risky international bond funds invest in bonds issued by foreign governments, or by stable foreign companies that focus on a number of industries, not just one. The riskiest international bond funds are those that invest in so-called emerging market countries, i.e., countries in Latin America, Asia, or Eastern Europe. The fund's prospectus will tell you exactly where the bond fund intends to put its money. The tricky part of investing in these funds is that whenever you invest abroad, your money (and thus your yield) is subject to the fluctuations of the currency markets as well as of interest rates. Your international bond fund will lose money if the value of the U.S. dollar increases against foreign currencies. Also, the interest rates of other countries cannot be predicted in the same way as those in the United States. I know of many people who have done well with the higher yields offered by international bond funds, but I also know people who have had some unpleasant surprises because of currency devaluation.

THE MATURITY FACTOR IN A BOND FUND

You mentioned that bond funds had no maturity dates. What about the maturity dates of individual bonds within the fund? Do they make a difference?

Yes, they do. Although your bond fund has no maturity date, the maturity dates of the individual bonds in your fund will have a big influence on your total returns. The longer the average maturity of the bonds in your fund, the greater the risk to you—or, rather, to the price of your shares—when interest rates fluctuate. The quality of the bonds in the portfolio also makes a big difference in regard to risk. The lower the quality of the bonds, the higher their yield, but the higher the risk as well. Because bond funds come in all sizes and shapes, you can have different kinds of funds that are sold under the name of a specific category of fund. For example, you can have a Treasury bond fund with bonds that have short-term maturities and one with bonds that have long-term maturities—each is a Treasury bond fund, but their share prices react very differently to a change in interest rates. You can see it is important to know not only what type of fund you might want to invest in, but also the characteristics of the specific fund as well.

What is a short-term bond fund?

Short-term in this context means that the bond fund typically owns bonds with average maturity dates of anywhere from one to five, and sometimes fewer, years. This doesn't necessarily mean that this bond fund only buys short-term bonds; it's simply an overall investing philosophy. In my opinion, short-term bond funds could be a good temporary shelter for your money, since it is unlikely that they will rise and fall dramatically with interest-rate fluctuations. Of course, since they are less risky than other kinds of investments, their yields will be lower. Still, they will generally outearn a CD or a money-market fund.

What is an intermediate-term bond fund?

It's a fund holding bonds whose average maturity date is from five to ten years. These funds can be quite a bit more volatile than short-term funds, though they are still generally considered less risky than long-term bond funds.

What is a long-term bond fund?

Its bonds have a typical maturity date of anywhere from 10 to 20 years or longer. Such bond funds usually pay the highest interest rates, but they can be extremely risky as well. Often, intermediate-term bond funds can provide investors with approximately the same total returns, with a lot less risk attached. I would not recommend long-term bond funds unless interest rates are extremely high and projected to come down. Even if this were the case, you would still be far better off, in my opinion, in long-term individual bonds.

How can I determine which of these terms is right for me?

As is often the case with bonds, the answer totally depends on what is happening with overall interest rates. If interest rates are about to go up and you are sure you want to buy a bond fund, then I suggest looking for one with very short-term maturities. If interest rates are relatively stable, an intermediate-term fund would be OK. And if interest rates are about to come down after a period of being very high, long-term funds might be the best choice. Remember, the longer the average maturity of the bonds within a bond fund, the more volatile the per-share price and the greater price fluctuations will be. Share prices will move farther downward when interest rates go up, and vice versa. Again, individual bonds of the same duration would probably accomplish your goals better than funds.

***How can I find out the length of the maturities of the
individual bonds in a bond fund?***

Morningstar, a mutual fund–rating service *(www.morningstar
.com),* lists the maturities of individual bonds in bond funds.

BUYER BEWARE

What do you think of bond funds?

As you have probably gathered, I am not a fan of bond funds.
If your aims are fixed income and the stability of your principal, bond funds are not the best way to go, especially if you
have $10,000 or more to invest. I believe the best bets are indi-
vidual bonds or stocks of stable companies that pay generous
dividends.

Many investment advisers will disagree with me about bond
funds. They will argue that you need a bond fund, especially if
you do not have a lot of money, because individual bonds
always carry a risk of defaulting. You need to protect yourself,
they say, by diversifying among a lot of bonds, which you
can't do if you don't have a lot of money. So they will tell you
to buy a bond fund. I understand their point of view, but I'm
not persuaded.

So I should never buy into a bond fund?

Well, bond funds have their uses. For example, if you have less
than $10,000 to invest, you need the highest current yield you
can get, and if yield is more important to you than knowing
that you will get your principal back in full, then you might
look into purchasing a bond fund instead of individual bonds.
Some people who need a monthly income prefer bond funds

to individual bonds because the funds offer monthly instead of semiannual income. Also, if for some reason you need cash in a hurry, you can write checks against the amount of your principal in a bond fund. I would advise against doing this, however, since whenever you do, you are selling off shares, and you will have to pay capital-gains taxes on any profits.

Safety through diversification, which they say is easy to come by with a fund, still sounds good to me.
In theory, it seems wise to want to diversify. However, while it is true that some individual bonds carry a risk of defaulting, not all bonds do. Treasuries, for instance, are the safest investment you can make. If you have a small sum of money that you want to invest in bonds, your investment does not have to be diversified as long as your money is absolutely safe. You could put every penny you have into a Treasury, regardless of your age, and your money would be secure from default. This may not be the wisest thing to do with respect to inflation risk, but it demonstrates that the reasoning that tells us the only way to be safe is to diversify by using a bond fund simply does not hold water.

What if I don't want to buy a Treasury? I am in the 28 percent tax bracket, and I would prefer to buy municipal bonds because I do not want to pay taxes on the interest.
We need to look at your financial situation more closely. The taxes on an investment of $10,000 or less in a taxable bond are not going to be that great. If you're in the 28 percent tax bracket, and you put $10,000 in a Treasury that earns 5 percent, then of the $500 you will earn in interest, $140 will go to the IRS in taxes, leaving you $360. If you were to put that same $10,000 in a municipal bond fund—let's say it paid you

3.5 percent—you would get $350 after taxes, less than the after-tax yield of the Treasury. With a Treasury, you know you will get back all $10,000 on the maturity date. With a bond fund, you do not have that assurance, because bond funds do not have a maturity date. Furthermore, if interest rates go up after you purchase the fund, you will not get back as much as you invested when you sell your shares. The bottom line is, what you earn in interest after taxes is essentially the same between the Treasury and the municipal bond fund ($360 vs. $350). The difference is that one guarantees your investment principal and the other guarantees nothing.

I have a lot more money than $10,000 to invest, and I do not want any more taxable income—so, in my case, wouldn't it make sense to buy a municipal bond fund?
The answer is still no. First of all, if you have a lot more money to invest, you can diversify by buying individual municipal bonds. Second, if your main desire is to avoid paying taxes, you have an even stronger reason to stay away from bond funds: There's one tax you may have to pay anyway. Most funds have an end-of-the-year capital-gains distribution. So even if you go into a municipal bond fund with the sole intention of never having to pay taxes while you own it, you may very well find you are paying taxes at the end of the year.

If I purchase a bond fund, will I have to pay capital-gains taxes at the end of the year, as I do with stock mutual funds?
All bond funds distribute capital gains, just as stock mutual funds do. In addition, bond funds reduce their share price by the amount of their distributions, just as stock funds do.

I bought my bond fund when interest rates were high. Why is my income going down with interest rates?

Because as new money comes into the fund, the portfolio manager buys bonds with this money. If interest rates have dropped since you invested your money, the bonds the fund manager is buying with the new money will have a lower yield. This will affect the overall yield of the bond portfolio, which in turn affects every shareholder's yield, including yours.

Can you summarize why you like individual bonds over bond funds?

Sure. Even though bond fund prices are supposed to go up when interest rates go down, and vice versa, it doesn't always happen that way. This makes bond funds unpredictable in spite of the fact that bonds are typically very predictable invest-ments. In addition, when interest rates go down, the interest rate that you are earning in a bond fund will also fall. If you are on a fixed income, this could be disastrous. Not only will you be getting less money monthly, but the offering price—that is, the price you could get for your shares—might stagnate or, worse, decline. Then you could really be in trouble. Also note that when you buy into a bond fund, you pay the current offering price of the fund on the day you place your order. You can tell your broker how much you want to spend, but you will not know for sure how many shares you will actually own until the fund closes for that day.

Imagine you've bought into a bond fund that is yielding 7.8 percent at a time when you could have bought an individual bond with a coupon, or interest rate of 7 percent. Let's say that you are retired and living on a fixed income. Although you could have locked in that 7 percent for the next ten years, when you bought your fund, you were told not to worry: If interest rates go down, your fund's value will increase. So you buy. Interest rates start to come down. You notice that your income is going down and the price per share of your bond fund is also declining. What is going on?

Well, it's the story I told just a moment ago. New investors are entering your mutual fund all the time, even as rates go down. The portfolio manager has to keep buying new bonds—at lower yields. This affects the rate of return for everyone who is in the fund. Also, as the fund prices start to go down, investors may start to pull their money out of the fund. If the manager does not have the cash to give them, he or she may have to liquidate bonds to raise cash. Depending on how the portfolio is invested, losses within the fund may have to be taken, and you will see the share price go down as well.

Meanwhile, if you had bought an individual bond when the interest rates were high, you would be reaping the rewards, since your yield is fixed and you would have seen the price of your bond increase. Why? You are not subject to new money being invested, and you do not have to worry about others liquidating, as you do in a fund. Furthermore, since bond funds do not have a maturity date, you are never guaranteed to get back your original investment. Individual bonds do have a maturity date, and in Treasuries you are always guaranteed to get back your principal investment.

Can you further summarize all the advantages of buying individual bonds over bond funds?
Yes. Here they are. With an individual bond:

- You know precisely the amount of money that you will get back at the maturity date.

- You will never have to pay end-of-the-year capital-gains taxes.
- You will not have to worry about the portfolio manager leaving. Nor will you have to worry about inside fees and expenses of the fund. If interest rates go down or up, you will most likely see an honest movement to the upside or downside.
- You will know your exact coupon rate, and it will never change, even if interest rates go down.
- You will know the exact price that you are paying per bond and the yield that you will be getting.

But if individual bonds are better for all these reasons, why do people buy into bond funds?

Because there are exceptions to everything—and that holds true for bond funds. As I've said, sometimes bond funds can be a good place to put money in the short term or even the intermediate term. However, for the long haul, when you are looking for a stable income and want control over your money, I would go with individual bonds. Make sure they have a safe rating, or stick with Treasuries.

If I happen to think I should still get a bond fund, do you have any tips on what to look out for?

The first thing I would look at is the load, or the sale commission. The way loads work on bond funds is identical to how they work on mutual funds. The only kind of bond fund I would want to see you buy would be a no-load fund. Again, no-load means no commission. You can buy or sell shares anytime you want, and it will not cost you a penny.

If I do buy a bond fund, does the expense ratio make a difference?

Yes, it makes a huge difference. Annual expense ratios come right off the total return of this fund. The higher the expense ratio, the lower your return. Be careful here and check.

If I decide to buy a bond fund, how much should I pay in management fees and expense ratios?

In a good fund, the management fee—that is, the fee paid to the person or team buying and selling the bonds in the fund—should be half a percent, give or take a fraction. If it's more than this, you've got a greedy manager. Please note: Every fund has charges in addition to the manager's fees. The expense ratio comprises all the fees the fund charges its investors. The expense ratio for a good bond fund should not be greater than 0.6 percent. The higher the expense ratio, the lower your yield.

MONEY-MARKET FUNDS

A money-market fund is simply a mutual fund that invests in liquid, safe debt instruments, such as short-term Treasuries. Money-market funds offer investors access to their money along with higher interest rates than are available from passbook or checking accounts—and, in many cases, at a cost that's far less than the monthly expense of a checking account.

My bank offers money-market deposit accounts. What are they, and should I consider one?

It's important not to mix up money-market funds with money-market deposit accounts, MMDAs, which are offered by banks and are insured up to $100,000 (up to $250,000, for retirement accounts under one name). As of this writing, bank MMDs offer better yields than bank savings accounts or money-market mutual funds, around 5.25 percent.

You say "funds." I didn't realize that there were different types of money-market funds.

There are four main types of such funds, and they deal in the debt obligations of the same four kinds of issuers that we've been talking about from the beginning of this chapter. They are:

- *U.S. Treasury funds.* These funds invest primarily in direct U.S. Treasury obligations whose principal and interest payments are backed by the full faith and credit of the U.S. government.
- *U.S. government funds.* These funds invest in high-quality obligations of agencies of the U.S. government as well as the U.S. Treasury. The full faith and credit of the U.S. government does not back agency securities.
- *General-purpose corporate funds.* These funds invest in the short-term debt of large, high-quality corporations and banks.
- *Tax-free money-market funds.* These funds invest in municipal bonds. You pay no federal taxes on your return on these investments, and no state tax, either, if you reside in the state in which the obligations are issued.

What is the best use of a money-market fund?

Use it as a parking place for money that you want to keep safe and/or for money that you know you will need within the next two years.

What questions should I ask myself before I open a money-market fund?

Here are a few: Have you got a sum of money that you want to keep safe and have easily available for spending? Do you want that money to be earning more interest than you can get from a savings account or a checking account? Do you want to stop paying $10 a month for check-writing privileges? If your answers are yes, start checking out money-market funds.

Why are money-market accounts so low-risk?

Because they typically invest in very short-term instruments of debt. By this I mean certificates of deposit (CDs), government notes, and T-bills with very short maturities—usually of 90 days. The best thing about money-market funds is their near guarantee that whatever money you put in, you will be able to get back out at any time, without penalty.

Uh-oh. What do you mean by "near guarantee"?

When you invest in a money-market fund, you buy shares—$1 for one share. The equation is supposed to remain constant, and history shows that it almost always does. On the very few occasions that the value of shares has dropped below $1, the funds have made good on the loss—despite the fact that they are not FDIC-insured.

What are some other advantages of investing in a money-market fund?

Again, since money-market funds invest primarily in short-term debt instruments, any risk due to changing interest rates is significantly lowered. Plus, the rules for diversifying money-market funds are far more rigorous than the rules governing diversified mutual funds that invest in stocks. No more than 25 percent of a regular mutual fund's assets can be put in a single investment. With money-market funds, the rule is no more than 5 percent. This ensures that if one or another investment starts to do poorly, the rest of the fund will not be seriously affected. Also, if a money-market fund invests in commercial paper—that is, corporate debt—a very high percentage of that debt instrument (almost 95 percent) has to be rated A1 by Standard & Poor's or Moody's, and if a money-market fund has invested in a debt instrument that carries a variable rate, the fund manager must ensure that the initial rate is solid enough so that if it wobbles, it won't affect the overall value of the fund. As you can see, money-market funds are designed to minimize risk and to provide you with protection from jiggly markets.

How do I start looking for a good money-market fund in which to invest?

I am glad that you said "invest," since it is important to remember that you are investing your money, not just putting it into a savings account at the bank. As with any kind of mutual fund, I would first read the fund's prospectus and any annual or quarterly reports you can get your hands on. Some of these can be downloaded right off the Internet. Second, I would check to see what kinds of debt instruments the money-market fund invests in. The least risk (and probably the lowest yields) would be in a fund invested in Treasury securities. You could probably find a higher yield (and a slightly higher risk) with a money-market fund that invested in Eurodollars or commercial paper, i.e., corporate debt. To find the money-market funds paying the best interest rates, check a financial magazine such as *Money* or *SmartMoney,* or the website *www.bankrate.com.* They list the best-performing money-market funds in the United States, along with their telephone numbers.

Is there anything else I should look out for?

As always, read the fine print. Find out if there is a minimum amount on your check-writing privilege, in case you need your money in a hurry. Does the fund offer wire or electronic transfers so you can get your money sooner rather than later? Is there a charge for writing a check or for withdrawing some of your money? Keep these things in mind.

How much cash do I need to open a money-market fund account?

You can usually open one with as little as $500 to $1,000.

Do I always get check-writing privileges with my money-market fund?

Not always, but usually.

Then why shouldn't I just transfer all the money in my checking account into my money-market account? That way I can earn higher interest but still have check-writing privileges.

Good question, but be careful. Most money-market accounts will permit you to write checks against your account balance, but many institutions set a limit on the number of checks you can write every month, or stipulate that the checks you write have to be in amounts of $250 or greater. Ask about this before setting up your account.

How else is a money-market fund account different from my regular bank account?

Bank accounts are insured by the FDIC; money-market funds are not. However, money-market funds generally pay higher interest rates and cost you far less in fees.

My bank offers a money-market fund to its depositors. If I take them up on the offer, will my money not be insured?

Here's an exception to what I said above. Banks have begun to offer money-market funds in order to compete with the mutual fund companies. These accounts are insured by the FDIC, but their yields tend to be a lot lower, because of the high cost of the banks' overhead.

I have a money-market fund with about $30,000 in it. Is there any danger in this?

Not with regard to the safety of your money. But there's another sort of risk—that the bank will start pestering you with offers you can't refuse, but should. If you have more than $5,000 or $10,000 in a money-market account, it is possible—probable, in fact—that someone representing the bank or brokerage firm where the money is kept will call you, offering to help you invest this money for a better rate of return. (Many banks now have in-house brokerage services to help their clients invest.) Obviously, the bank or brokerage firm will make more money in the long run if you invest this money in certain ways rather than others. So these companies keep an eye on accounts with a consistent stash of cash, in the hope that if they call you, you will be open to listening to their ideas. Please be careful if this happens. Don't do anything you don't want to do. It's your money. Just keep in mind, and tell them, that your goal with these funds is to keep them safe and sound and available in case of an emergency.

CERTIFICATES OF DEPOSIT (CDs)

Certificates of deposit, or CDs, are a type of savings instrument issued by a bank or a credit union (or even a broker). Like individual bonds, they pay you a specified rate of interest over a specified period of time, and pay back your principal at maturity.

Are CDs insured by the Fed?
CDs are insured up to $100,000. The Fed will not insure anything over this ceiling, unless the money is held in a retirement account. Funds up to $250,000 in a retirement account will be insured. Granted, banks don't make a habit of going belly-up, but you want to cover your assets in a worst-case scenario, so keep that $100,000/$250,000 limit in mind.

Why should one invest in a CD?
Like money-market funds, CDs are a very safe, very conservative part of an investment portfolio. I think CDs are a very good place to park savings you might be holding for an expense you anticipate in the near term, or until you decide what you are going to do with them on a long-term basis. However, I would not recommend keeping the lion's share of your money in CDs, unless it is the only place where you feel your money is safe and sound, and you need current income.

Should I buy a CD from the bank where I keep my checking and savings accounts, or is it worth my while to shop around?

I would certainly inquire at your bank whether or not the fact that you are already a customer affects the rate of the CD (and also whether opening a CD may lower your banking fees). Sometimes banks favor their long-term customers and customers with larger combined balances. If the answer is no, then I would shop around for the best rate.

What is the most important thing for me to keep in mind as I shop for a CD?

The first thing I would want to know is what the CD's maturity is. The next thing to find out is the current interest rate. For a list of current CDs, and their maturities and rates, log on to *www.bankrate.com.*

Will I be penalized if I take my money out of a CD before the maturity date?

Yes. You will usually be charged an early-withdrawal penalty (EWP). Check with the bank that's offering the CD to find out how much this penalty is, as it varies.

Do all banks penalize customers if they withdraw their money early from a CD?

The majority of them do, but I've noticed that more and more banks are now waiving the EWP. This waiver has a price, however: lower interest rates. So you have to ask yourself whether or not it's worth it. Better yet, decide beforehand, to the best of your knowledge, if you might need this money before the maturity date. None of us can predict the future or those times when life will throw us a curveball, but you can certainly prepare for uncertainty—for example, by buying CDs in smaller denominations and/or staggering their maturity dates. If you invested $80,000 in a CD and for some reason you decided to take your money out early because you needed just $10,000, the bank would charge you an EWP on all $80,000. Wouldn't it have been just as easy—and in the end, cheaper—to have bought eight certificates of deposit at $10,000 apiece? This way, if you need emergency money and want to cash out one of your CDs, the bank will levy an EWP on a CD of only $10,000.

What other questions should I ask?

I would ask about variable-rate CDs. Depending on the interest-rate climate, these may offer higher or lower returns than a fixed-rate CD. If you think that interest rates are bound to rise in the near future, then you should definitely think about putting your money in a variable-rate CD. It allows you to take advantage of rising rates and protects you, by its withdrawal features, in case rates fall or you need access to your funds. I've already mentioned the advantages of staggering your maturity dates. This means that you have one CD that comes to maturity in six months, another that comes to maturity in a year, etc. This acts as a partial protection against interest-rate fluctuations.

Most important, find out about the rate of return (the annual percentage yield, or APY). Interest rates are dependent on the maturity of the CD, and they also vary from bank to bank.

Finally, you should also ask how often interest is paid or credited to your CD. Is it daily? Monthly? Quarterly? The more often it is credited to your account, the better for you.

Are brokers useful here?

Actually, I recommend buying CDs through a broker. Yes, you read that right! Some CDs that are bought through your broker have one big advantage that CDs bought from a bank do not have: They can be sold (and bought) on the secondary market. Let's say you bought a five-year CD, and six months into it you need your money. Rather than taking an automatic interest-rate hit or an EWP, you can instruct your broker to sell your CD for you on the secondary market. If interest rates have fallen since you purchased your CD, you could get back more than you invested. (This is because another investor may be willing to pay a premium for the higher interest rate attached to your CD.) If they have stayed the same, you could get back what you put in; if they have risen, you could get back less. In any case, you will probably come out better than you would at the bank. And a brokerage firm can shop the whole country for you to find you the best rate or a buyer, if necessary. So check it out, for this may be one time a broker is worth consulting.

What is an "odd-term" CD?

An odd-term CD has an unconventional time period until maturity—for example, five months or seventeen months—as opposed to the standard six-month maturity.

What is a "step-up" CD?

A step-up CD allows you to lock in the current interest rate and take advantage of rising rates during the term of the CD—usually between one and five years—by converting to the higher yield without penalty. Most banks will allow you to step up to a higher rate once during the term of the CD, but you must notify the bank to initiate the step-up process; it does not automatically occur once rates change.

Do you think buying a Treasury note is better than buying a CD?

There are pluses and minuses to both CDs and Treasury notes. Treasury notes pay you interest that's not taxed at the local or state level. Any interest that you make on your CD is taxable at the local and state levels, as well as at the federal level. So the bottom line depends on your tax bracket and the interest-rate difference. Overall, I prefer Treasuries to CDs because of the tax advantages and government guarantees. Also, you can invest far more than $100,000 in a Treasury note and still have your money safe and sound.

BUYER BEWARE: ANNUITIES

Annuities are controversial investments, even within the financial community. It's important to understand what annuities are and how they work, for without a doubt—and probably sooner rather than later—a broker or insurance agent will try to sell you one. Although there are circumstances in which buying an annuity may make sense, in a majority of cases I believe that annuities cause more harm than good.

All annuities are contracts with an insurance company for a specified period of time. But annuities are not really life insurance policies; for one thing, they do not include an extra death benefit payable to heirs. They are *investment* contracts, and as such must be compared to other investment vehicles, such as bank CDs and mutual funds. Annuities have one advantage over other investment vehicles outside a retirement plan, however, and this is what makes them so popular and such an easy sell: The money they earn for you, whether in interest or in increased value, is tax-deferred until you withdraw it. In this respect, annuities behave very much like nondeductible IRAs or even like 401(k)s, so they also have to be compared with retirement-savings vehicles. They are complicated. In most cases, you are penalized for withdrawing your money from an annuity until the surrender period expires *and* until you're 59½ or older; but you can always choose what's known as an "annuitization" option that lets you start taking a lifetime income—at a price. Most annuities also carry an ongoing price in the form of special annual charges and fees that come straight out of your annuity account—and therefore out of any profit.

Frankly, I take a dim view of annuities. Yet in a few cases, they make excellent financial sense. In the following sections, I've made clear what those cases are and also the major drawbacks in most other cases—perhaps even yours. If you already own an annuity, this chapter will give you the tools to evaluate it and—should you decide you want to extricate yourself—to avoid mistakes when disposing of it.

ANNUITY BASICS

What is an annuity?

An annuity is an investment contract or policy between you (the policyholder) and an insurance company. There are many kinds of annuities. Some are tailored for income, some for growth, some as savings vehicles. All offer tax-deferred growth of your earnings within the policy or account. None, however, offer an additional death benefit, and this makes them very different from a life insurance policy. Also unlike an insurance policy, an annuity is purchased with a single lump-sum payment; the minimum investment in a typical annuity is about

$5,000. Depending on what kind of annuity you buy, in return for your investment the insurance company will provide you with certain contractual guarantees—for example, it will guarantee a minimum rate of return over the life of the contract and/or a guaranteed interest rate for any given year. Such guarantees are one of the reasons annuities are popular and are widely believed to be safe investments.

Can you remind me what tax-deferred means?

It means that you put off paying taxes—in this case, taxes on the interest or other earnings in your account—until you start making withdrawals at age 59½ or older (or, in the event of your death, until your beneficiaries withdraw the investment and the earnings). The advantage of tax deferral is that money you would otherwise pay in taxes every year is allowed to remain in your account, earning additional interest or creating further gains. In the arena of tax deferral, annuities function very much like some IRAs. In essence, they act as a tax shelter, and this is one of their big draws.

When an annuity is part of a qualified retirement plan, it is referred to as a "qualified" annuity and has one added tax benefit: Your initial investment, or premium, is also tax-deferred. But most annuities are "nonqualified" annuities and offer tax deferral only on the interest and other earnings that accrue in your account.

Can you elaborate on the difference between a qualified and a nonqualified annuity?

If you are investing with money on which you have already paid taxes, you are buying a nonqualified annuity. If you're investing with pretax money within a qualified retirement account, such as a 401(k), or as a rollover from a qualified retirement account, then you are buying a qualified annuity. Typically, you buy a qualified annuity within a retirement plan at work or as a transfer of money from a 401(k) or 403(b) plan.

Is it a good idea to own an annuity within my retirement plan?

I'm glad you asked this question. The answer is, usually not. Although brokers often try to sell annuities as investments within retirement plans, for the most part I see this as a bad idea. What sense does it make to hold a tax-sheltered product, such as an annuity, in an already tax-sheltered account, such as a 401(k) or an IRA? Not a lot.

Are there exceptions to this rule? Yes. Apart from being offered a particular type of annuity called a tax-sheltered annuity as part of your retirement plan at work, in my opinion the *only* two reasons to purchase an annuity in a retirement plan are the following:

- You are under the age of 59½, need to get access to the funds in your traditional IRA, and want to avoid paying the 10 percent early-withdrawal penalty tax levied by the IRS on withdrawals made before age 59½. By purchasing what's called an immediate, or income, annuity within your traditional IRA, you can receive monthly income right away *and* avoid the 10 percent IRS penalty tax.

- You are approaching retirement age, and you want to invest in the stock market but are afraid of losing your principal. You are willing to take a smaller potential profit in exchange for a guarantee against any losses. In this case, you might consider an index annuity, which lets you participate in stock-market gains on a limited basis while completely protecting you against losses. This strategy can make sense either inside or outside an IRA.

Again, my general advice is to steer clear of investing in annuities in a retirement plan.

Can I cancel an annuity, or take my money out, anytime I want to?

No. Once you buy an annuity contract, you're pretty much locked in. For one thing, if you take your money out of an annuity before you turn 59½, the IRS will impose its 10 percent early-withdrawal penalty tax. (In exchange for the privilege of tax deferral on the earnings in an annuity, the IRS limits your access to that money until you reach what the agency considers to be retirement age.) This penalty tax will come on top of the ordinary income taxes you will owe on any earnings in the account.

Second, the majority of annuity contracts contain what is known as a surrender period. This is a specified period of time—usually five to ten years—during which you must keep the greater part of your money in the account, even if you're already 59½ and are off the hook as far as the IRS is concerned. If you don't honor the surrender period, the insurance company will levy surrender charges. Those charges typically start at about 5 to 7 percent of the amount of the withdrawal and drop to zero by the time the surrender period is over. Most contracts *will* allow you to withdraw about 10 percent of the accumulated value of the account each year (after you are 59½) without a surrender charge, even during the surrender period. But if you withdraw more than 10 percent a year, you will pay a surrender charge on the amount that you withdraw in excess of 10 percent.

Let me give you an example. Let's say you are 60 years old

and have put $50,000 into an annuity. Say the annuity is paying you a guaranteed annual interest rate of 5 percent a year for the five-year duration of the contract. At the end of the third year, your annuity is worth $57,881. Suddenly you find you need $7,000. You can withdraw 10 percent of the $57,881, or $5,788, without any penalty whatsoever. Withdrawing the additional $1,212, however, will cost you approximately $60, based on a surrender charge of 5 percent. And since the IRS has funny rules about annuities, for tax purposes the entire amount of your early withdrawal will be considered to have come from the earnings portion of the account. So you will also owe ordinary income tax on the whole $7,000.

Please note: If you were 40 rather than 60 years old and needed $7,000, you would owe the IRS a 10 percent early-withdrawal penalty tax—or $700—plus ordinary income taxes.

Do all annuities have a surrender charge?

Most do, but not all. No-load annuities, such as those offered by The Vanguard Group, do not carry brokers' commissions or sales charges, and Vanguard's variable deferred annuity has no surrender charges, either..

Are annuities federally insured, as bank CDs are?

No, annuities are not federally insured. If for some reason the insurance company from which you've purchased an annuity flounders or goes belly-up, your annuity account can be frozen and/or reduced in value.

What if I want to change the insurance company I hold my annuity with? Can I switch?

Yes. In most cases, the IRS allows what is known as a 1035 exchange between insurance companies (the exception is an immediate, or income, annuity). A 1035 exchange lets you switch companies while continuing to defer taxes. You can either fill out exchange paperwork with your original insurance company or create a new contract with a new insurance company and let the new company take care of the transfer. Don't switch before the end of the surrender period, however, if you can help it; if you do, you may have to pay the surrender charge. The surrender charge will probably be deducted before the money is transferred, reducing the amount you have available for reinvestment.

Can you tell me about the annuity contract?

Yes. For every annuity contract, there is an *owner,* an *annuitant,* and a *beneficiary.* This is a little complicated, so bear with me.

The *owner* of the contract is the person who purchases the contract or policy. The owner owns the policy, and is entitled to make changes in the beneficiary designation on the policy at any time. The owner can also "annuitize" the policy, which basically means choosing to take a monthly income for life instead of leaving the annuity to beneficiaries or taking a lump-sum payment at age 59½ or older. (I'll say more about this later, but annuitizing is not always a good deal.) When two or more people own a policy together, they are known as co-owners. The owner or co-owners can also name a successor owner, someone they designate to step in as owner in the event of the owners' death or, in some cases, incapacity.

The *annuitant* is the insured party—which may seem odd in an investment contract that has no additional death benefit. But in order for an annuity to qualify as a legitimate insurance contract, which is what makes possible its tax advantages, someone has to be insured. Usually the insured person is also the owner; if the annuitant is *not* the owner, he or she has no power over the money in the account.

The annuitant becomes important if and when you choose to annuitize your contract. In that case, the monthly income you receive will be determined not by your own age but by the annuitant's age and life expectancy. For example, if I bought an annuity and named my mother the annuitant, she would qualify for much more money each month than I would if I were the annuitant. The older the annuitant is and the shorter his or her life expectancy, the larger the monthly payments; this makes sense if you consider that the insurance company is predicting that it will have to make fewer payments to an older person.

The *beneficiary* is the person (or people) whom you, as owner, designate to inherit whatever is left in the annuity when the annuitant (who may be you) dies. Remember, every annuity must have a named beneficiary (even though, in some cases, if you choose to "annuitize" an annuity, your beneficiary won't inherit anything; most annuitization payments end with the annuitant's death). The owner decides how much to leave each beneficiary. The beneficiary and the annuitant cannot be the same person, but when the owner and annuitant are separate, the owner and the beneficiary can be the same person. So, for example, if I buy an annuity insuring my mother, I could be named the beneficiary on her death. Usually, however, the owner and the annuitant are the same person, and often a spouse or a child is the beneficiary.

PURCHASING AN ANNUITY

How do I buy an annuity?

Typically, you buy an annuity directly from an insurance company. You can also buy an annuity through a brokerage firm or discount brokerage firm or, in some cases, through a bank or mutual fund company.

Are there commission charges when I buy an annuity?

Typically, yes. Except for annuities offered by no-load mutual fund companies such as Vanguard Group, most annuities carry a load, or commission percentage, of about 5 or 6 percent.

How do I choose an insurance company from which to purchase an annuity?

Start by looking at how the insurance companies you have in mind are rated for financial strength by the following insurance-rating services. The only acceptable ratings are:

A.M. Best—A or better
(908) 439-2200   *www.ambest.com*

Moody's—A or better
(212) 553-0377   *www.moodys.com*

Standard & Poor's—AA or better
(212) 438-2000   *www.standardandpoors.com*

Duff & Phelps—AA or better
(312) 263-2610   *www.fitchratings.com*

Ask each insurance company to give you written notification of its ratings when it sends you its prospective materials, or call the ratings companies directly.

If I like the company's ratings, what else should I look for in an insurance company?

Here are a few more things to bear in mind when shopping for an annuity. Take a look at the quality of the investments held by the insurance company, because the company's investments can affect the return you get on your investment. If more than 10 percent of your insurance company's total invested holdings are junk bonds, meaning bonds that have a rating of BB or lower, be wary.

How can I get all this information? Presumably, the insurance companies themselves won't volunteer it.

Actually, insurance companies will provide this information if you ask. Many publish their ratings and holdings in a brochure or in a corporate annual report.

Besides checking into the safety of the issuing insurance company, how do I know if an annuity is a good deal or not?

Whether an annuity is a good deal for you will depend on your financial goals, your tax bracket, and the type of annuity you are considering.

KINDS OF ANNUITIES

Today, for all practical purposes, there are six major kinds of annuities available for purchase: a single-premium deferred annuity; a variable annuity; an index annuity; a split annuity; an immediate, or income, annuity; and a tax-sheltered annuity. When the time comes to withdraw your investment from an annuity, most of these let you either take a lump sum or convert your investment into a monthly income payment for life—an option known as "annuitization." Here's what you need to know about the basic kinds of annuities and how to withdraw your money from them.

SINGLE-PREMIUM DEFERRED ANNUITIES

What is a single-premium deferred annuity?

A single-premium deferred annuity, or SPDA, is a fixed annuity that you buy with a single premium. You get a guaranteed interest rate for a specified period of time, and the taxes on the interest you earn are deferred until you make a withdrawal.

Who would want to buy an SPDA?

Anyone who wants to let his or her money grow risk-free while deferring income taxes on the earnings portion of his or her account, with the goal of creating income later in life, may choose an SPDA. Many people enjoy the idea of a fixed interest rate that will remain in effect for a specified period of time, typically from one to seven years. In most cases, the longer the guarantee, the lower the interest rate. This type of annuity is most easily compared to a certificate of deposit at a bank. In both cases, you get a guaranteed rate for a prescribed period. In an annuity, you incur surrender charges if you take your money out, and in a CD you are faced with a three- to six-month early-withdrawal penalty. The difference, however, is that with a certificate of deposit, you will be paying taxes each year on the interest you earn, even if you don't withdraw it. With the SPDA, you will not pay taxes until you make a withdrawal.

Are you in favor of SPDAs, or should I steer clear of them?

I do like SPDAs for some people. You might consider an SPDA if:

- Your goal is to invest money with minimal risk, and you are attracted to vehicles such as CDs and Treasuries; and
- You know you are not going to need any of the money you're investing until after age 59½; and
- You do not need current income but will need income sometime after age 59½ and will be in an equal or lower tax bracket; or
- You are already 59½ or older, you need current income, and the SPDA you are considering offers a guaranteed five-year interest rate that is higher than the interest on five-year CDs and Treasuries.

In summary, there is one set of circumstances in which I would definitely advise you to consider an SPDA. If your goal is to have income during your retirement years but you don't want to take any market risk with your capital, *and* you want to avoid paying taxes now but are not in a high enough tax bracket for municipal bonds to make sense, *and* you believe that you will be in a lower tax bracket when you retire, then an SPDA may be a great investment, regardless of your age.

I also recommend an SPDA when someone is under age 59½ and needs to take SEPPs (substantially equal periodic payments) for income (payments you can take without paying a 10 percent IRS penalty tax).

What should I watch out for when shopping for an SPDA?

The first step you should take is to check to be sure the insurance company issuing the annuity is safe. Next, and this is very important, ask about the interest rate being offered, the period of time during which the interest rate will be guaranteed, and the surrender period stipulated by the contract. Ideally, the interest rate should be a good one, and the period for which the rate is guaranteed should be at least as long as the surrender period. (In other words, if the interest rate is 7 percent and the contract has a five-year surrender period, the company should pay you 7 percent for all five years.) If you are offered an attractive interest rate for a guaranteed one-year period but the surrender period goes on for seven years, please be wary. Even if the first-year rate is *outstanding,* in the absence of a longer guarantee you are taking a big risk as to what the interest rate will be for the second year, the third year, and so on. Many companies sucker you in with a good first-year rate and then lower it considerably in the remaining years. Finally, ask how the company sets its renewal interest rate, if applicable, or do some checking on your own. That way you know exactly what you are getting.

How can I check on a company's renewal rates?

Ask to see the history of renewal rates for older SPDA policies that the company has in force. If the company tends to lower the interest rates on policies as they get older, chances are good it will reduce yours, too. Make sure you compare the company's renewal rates in previous years to the rate on Treasuries and CDs for the same years. That way, you'll know whether it makes sense for you to purchase a particular SPDA.

I know that the IRS will allow me to switch my annuity from one insurance company to another. Is it ever worthwhile to transfer money to an SPDA at a new company if you are still in the surrender period?

Yes, if the new interest rate in the new company makes up for what you paid in surrender charges in the first year or two, then it may be worthwhile.

When my surrender period is up, I don't have to change my SPDA, do I?

No, although some insurance agents will make it sound as though you do—because if you switch, the agent earns a new commission. In general, if you are pleased with your current interest rate, stay where you are. Be careful: When you sign a new annuity contract, you start a new surrender period. And be sure to check on the new company's renewal rate history.

Can I annuitize my SPDA?

Yes, although it might not be wise to do so. Insurance companies that offer annuities tend to use different annuitization factors when annuitizing—that is, when calculating how much to pay you on a monthly basis over your life span. If you're looking for income from an annuity, it would be best to find out which companies are offering the best annuitization rates and/ or to buy outright an immediate, or income, annuity. Typically, the annuitization rates offered by SPDA contracts are not as advantageous as those offered by immediate annuity contracts, and even immediate annuity rates vary from company to company.

VARIABLE ANNUITIES

With billions of investors' dollars pouring into traditional mutual funds, insurance companies are offering a competing product called a variable annuity, which combines elements of an annuity with elements of mutual fund investing. For many reasons, including high fees and benefits that in my opinion are routinely overstated by salespeople, variable annuities are an investment I often warn against. If you are considering buying one, please read this section thoroughly. If you are still tempted, please do your homework and shop around for a no-load variable annuity.

What is a variable annuity?

Like other annuities, a variable annuity is a contract with an insurance company for a specific period of time. However, unlike some other annuities, a variable annuity does not offer a guaranteed rate of interest or earnings. In some ways, it is more like a 401(k) or an IRA; for example, when you buy a variable annuity, you are asked to choose from a menu of mutual funds within the insurance contract in which to invest your money. A variable annuity may offer a broad selection of funds or just a few to choose from, depending on which insurance company you go through. You can buy, sell, and switch funds at any time without incurring taxes until you begin to withdraw your original investment and income after age 59½. At that time, your gains are taxed as ordinary income.

How is a variable annuity different from an IRA?

Unlike many IRAs, a typical variable annuity cannot be funded with pretax dollars. It is a nonqualified annuity. In other words, you make your initial investment with money on which you've already paid ordinary income taxes. A variable annuity and an IRA *are* the same in that the earnings that accrue to your original investment over the years are tax-deferred until you withdraw them after age 59½. But this tax-deferral feature is typically less valuable in a variable annuity than in an IRA. I'll explain this later.

How is a variable annuity different from a single-premium deferred annuity?

When you buy an SPDA, your premium is deposited in the insurance company's general account. This account represents the assets of the company, and the company's financial experts decide how to invest the money and offer you a guaranteed rate of return. When you buy a variable annuity, your money is placed in what is known as a "separate account." Within limits, you decide where to invest. The insurance company gives you a menu of investment options, in the form of different mutual funds; you choose which funds to invest in and what percentage of your money will go in each of the funds you choose. As a result, your return is not guaranteed, and you are subject to a certain amount of investment risk.

What if I can't figure out which funds to choose?

Many people share your dilemma, so insurance companies typically offer something called an asset-allocation fund. This is a mutual fund that decreases investment risk (and also decreases potential rewards) by allocating your money in a range of investments, or assets, including stocks, bonds, Treasury bills, and more. This provides a relatively stable, though not entirely risk-free, choice.

Are there any very safe places to park my money in a variable annuity?

Yes. Many variable annuities have a fixed, or interest-bearing, fund as one of their investment offerings, so you can simply choose (or switch into) that one.

What are the advantages of variable annuities over regular mutual funds?

One of the big attractions of all annuities, including variable annuities, is that you enjoy tax deferral on your earnings. Even if you switch—that is, buy and sell—the mutual funds you hold within a variable annuity every day, you won't have to pay taxes on your realized gains until you actually withdraw money from the annuity. This is a great benefit, especially when compared with the tax policy on regular mutual funds you may be holding outside a variable annuity or other tax-deferred account. When you have large gains in an ordinary investment account, you may hesitate to sell the fund because you'd immediately owe capital-gains taxes on your earnings. If you invested in the same mutual fund within a variable annuity, you could sell it and not pay taxes until you withdrew money. When you do make a withdrawal, however, your gains will be taxed not at the low capital-gains rate, but as ordinary income.

Second, at the end of the year mutual funds have what is known as an end-of-the-year capital-gains distribution. With a variable annuity, you will not have to pay taxes on your end-of-the-year distributions at that time.

Finally, an advantage of most variable annuities is that they guarantee that the owner or beneficiaries of the annuity will get back *at least* the amount of the initial investment when the annuitant in the contract (the insured party) dies. In other words, no matter what happens to the particular mutual funds in which you choose to invest your premium, when the annuitant in your contract dies, you (the owner) or your heirs will not receive less than the amount you originally invested *or* the current value of the account, whichever is greater. In a regular mutual fund, there is no such guarantee. But hold your horses! In most cases, this so-called benefit is less valuable than you might think, and it is not without cost. Soon we'll discuss the downside of variable annuities, which you should keep in mind as you consider buying one.

Does this mean that a variable annuity is a good way to invest in the market without having to worry about losses or taxes?

No. While it's true that there is some security in the guarantee described above and an attractive short-term benefit in tax deferral on earnings, in my opinion, a variable annuity that *is* profitable will not save you much in taxes over the long run—which, for most people who buy a variable annuity, is the point of owning one.

Are there fees that I have to pay with a variable annuity that I wouldn't have to pay with mutual funds held outside of an annuity?

Yes. Remember that an annuity shelters the growth of your money from immediate taxation because it is considered an insurance product. For it to qualify as such, there has to be someone who is insured—the annuitant. Most variable annuities carry what is called a mortality fee, which is associated with the risks attached to the death of the annuitant. This fee is not charged by mutual funds outside a variable annuity. Many variable annuities also charge application fees and additional expenses that do not exist in a regular mutual fund. Finally, you also have to pay the expense ratio (typically, from one percent to two percent a year) that mutual funds levy, whether they are within a variable annuity or not.

How big is the mortality fee?

A mortality fee will typically cost you 1.3 percent of your investment a year, or $13 a year for every $1,000 that you invest. Insurance companies justify the fee by claiming it is necessary to cover the cost of the guarantee they give you against losing any of your money when the annuitant, or insured party in your contract, dies. (Remember, one attraction of variable annuities is that the owner and/or the named beneficiaries are guaranteed to get back the full amount of the original investment *or* the account value at the time of the annuitant's death, whichever is greater; this is what this fee covers.) But here's the fallacy: In most cases, the owner and the annuitant are one and the same person—you. If this is the case, you don't benefit at all from the guarantee, and you lose out by paying the mortality fee. Here's why: Say you need your money—you want to withdraw it all and close the account— while you are alive. If your balance happens to be less than you originally deposited, you are out of luck. You will have lost money. The guarantee only applies in the case of the annuitant's death. If you are the annuitant, a lot of good this guarantee—for which you have been paying dearly—does you. However, if you *don't* need your money before you die, the guarantee may benefit your family after you are gone.

Tell me about the tax disadvantages of a variable annuity.

One serious disadvantage of variable annuities is relative—that is, the tax *advantages* they promise are not always everything they're cracked up to be. Most variable annuities are sold with the promise that you'll not only get a long-term tax deferral on your gains, but you will also save a lot of money in taxes on (1) end-of-the-year mutual fund distributions, and (2) gains on which you would otherwise be taxed everytime you buy and sell a mutual fund. But you don't need a variable annuity to avoid paying taxes on end-of-the-year distributions; you can accomplish the same end outside an annuity with a good tax-efficient mutual fund, such as an index fund, or with an exchange-traded mutual fund, or ETF. As to item (2), most people don't regularly buy and sell mutual funds, especially index funds; they hold on to them for years. So if you have a tax-efficient mutual fund that you do not sell, then the truth is that you do not have a tax problem.

What about the long-term tax deferral that a variable annuity offers? Well, that's not so hot, either. Remember, when you withdraw your money after age 59½ you will have to pay taxes on the earnings portion of your annuity account. However, the earnings on your annuity, which constitute the tax-deferred part, are subject to ordinary income taxes rather than to the lower capital-gains taxes that you would owe if you owned an ordinary mutual fund outside an annuity account. If you hold your money in the same mutual fund outside an annuity for longer than 12 months, you will only have to pay taxes at the lower capital-gains rate (up to 15 percent as of 2007) rather than at the ordinary income rate (up to 35 percent as of 2007).

OK, you say, no big deal about the tax rate. You plan to leave the annuity to your children. But such a strategy merely shifts the tax burden to your kids—and at a steep price. When they withdraw money, they, too, will owe income taxes on the growth of your funds (which could be considerable) at ordinary income-tax rates, plus they will have to pay a state premium tax, if applicable, of about 2 percent of your original deposit. If you had simply purchased mutual funds directly and left them to your children via a will or trust, they would get what is called a step-up in cost basis on the value of those funds, based on the funds' worth on the day you died. If they then sold those funds before there was a further increase in the funds' value, they would not owe a penny in taxes.

Another disadvantage: If you lose money in a variable annuity account in any given year, you can't deduct any of your losses from your taxes, but you can deduct any losses you take or any distributed losses if you have the money in a mutual fund outside of an annuity or in a retirement account.

If I have a loss in my variable annuity, can I take it off of my taxes?

If the variable annuity is part of a payout in a qualified plan, then the loss can be taken off your taxes, subject to a 2 percent threshold rule.

Can you give me an example of how placing regular mutual funds in a trust might be better for my heirs than buying an annuity would be?

Yes. Imagine that you have invested $25,000 in a variable annuity and that by the time you die, your investment has grown to be worth $125,000. Your children inherit the annuity and withdraw the money. They will owe ordinary income taxes on $100,000 in capital gains, along with state premium taxes, if applicable. Depending on their income-tax bracket, they might owe as much as 42 percent of the gain in your annuity.

Let's imagine that you put that same $25,000 into a few really good, tax-efficient mutual funds. When you die, your kids inherit the funds. If the funds were worth $125,000 on the day of your death, then $125,000 is your children's new cost basis for tax purposes. If on the following day they were to liquidate the funds and withdraw all $125,000 from the account, they would not owe a single penny in income taxes, since the funds have not increased in value since your death. If the funds did increase in value—say, to $127,000—they would owe taxes on a mere $2,000. This step-up in cost basis applies to inherited investments such as mutual funds, real estate, and stocks—but not to annuities, traditional IRAs, and retirement plans.

Can you give me an example of how I might be better off investing in a mutual fund outside an annuity account?

Yes. Let's look at the end-result difference between investing $100,000 in a variable annuity and investing $100,000 in a mutual fund outside an annuity.

Say you put $100,000 in a variable annuity. You have chosen an index fund within the annuity, and you have left your money in the fund for the 25 years without ever having touched one penny. You have averaged a 12 percent annual return, not taking into account the annual fees charged by the insurance company.

Let's see how you would fare in the variable annuity after all the insurance company's fees are taken out.

Your $100,000 at 12 percent a year over 25 years, minus a 1.3 percent mortality fee per year and a 0.2 percent expense fee per year, equals $1,213,547.

Now let's say you die and leave your entire account balance to your kids. You all live in the state of California. Your kids will have to pay state and federal income taxes on about $1,113,547 in earnings as though it were ordinary income, and they will have to pay a state premium tax of about $2,500.

Let's say your children take the money out in one lump sum. Between federal and state taxes, they would owe about $500,000 in taxes. So when it is all said and done, your children would end up receiving about $700,000.

OK, now let's see what would happen if you had purchased the same index fund in a regular account instead of an annuity. This is how it would look to your kids.

First of all, your children would inherit close to $1.7 million instead of $1.2 million, simply because you would not have had to pay the annual 1.3 percent mortality fee or the extra annual or 0.2 percent expense fee attached to the annuity. Believe it or not, after 25 years, that 1.5 percent per year subtracts about $500,000 from your annuity account.

Now you die and the kids receive all $1.7 million. Since they inherited your index fund instead of cash, they will get a step-up in cost basis to the $1.7 million mark. If they cash the fund out at that valuation, they will not owe one penny in taxes, so they will possess $1.7 million to use as they choose.

With a variable annuity, they would have $700,000. Without a variable annuity, they would have $1,700,000. You decide.

Do you think it's better to buy mutual funds outside a variable annuity and give up the advantage of tax deferral?

Yes—*if* you invest in tax-efficient mutual funds that help you to avoid a big annual tax bite *and* hold your mutual funds for longer than a year, so that your earnings qualify for the lower long-term capital-gains tax rate. This way, your tax bill won't be substantially higher, and you'll be able to gain access to your money anytime, at any age, without worrying about a 10 percent IRS early-withdrawal penalty tax or an insurance company surrender charge.

Is there any way to take money out of a variable annuity and still take advantage of its no-loss guarantee via the mortality charge that I have been paying for?

Yes. If you need to withdraw money from a variable annuity at a time when it's worth less than the amount you deposited, what you can do is this: Leave the account open, but withdraw most of your money. This way, when you die, your beneficiaries will receive the difference between what you have withdrawn and the guaranteed amount.

Let me give you an example. Say you deposit $25,000 into a variable annuity. You are the owner and the annuitant. Sometime later, you need money. When you go to cash out, the account is worth only $19,000. You withdraw $18,000, leaving $1,000 in the annuity. Years later, you die. Your beneficiaries will get $7,000. Remember, you have continued to pay the mortality fee of 1.3 percent of your original deposit amount each year to guarantee that on your death your beneficiaries will get back 100 percent of the original deposit, or the current worth of the account, whichever is greater. In this case, your original deposit of $25,000 is greater. Since you withdrew $18,000 before dying, the insurance company will owe your beneficiaries an additional $7,000.

Did the guarantee help you while you were alive? No. Were you able to take the loss in your account off your taxes, or use it to offset a gain? No. And what if you hadn't died in a few years? How long would the remaining money have had to sit in your account, losing value? For a long time, perhaps, even as the annual mortality fee and other charges continued to accrue.

Do I think that paying the mortality fee to protect your deposit is worth it? No, I do not.

Are there special disadvantages to a variable annuity in a bear market?

Yes. Even if you decide to hedge any stock-market losses by investing in or switching to a money-market fund within your variable annuity, the fees and charges you will pay on your annuity account diminish your return. Therefore, your return will not be as great as it would be in a money-market fund outside a variable annuity.

I'm considering buying a variable annuity to hold in my retirement account. Is this a good idea?

No! As a rule, buying any annuity to hold in a retirement account is a bad idea, and a variable annuity is no exception. The problem, in a nutshell, is this: You are buying a tax-deferred investment product to hold within a tax-deferred investment *account*, and so you are paying for the benefit of an extra layer of tax protection that you don't need. The price you pay for that extra tax deferral is about 1.5 to 2 percent of your annuity balance every year in fees and charges.

On the next page is a quick comparison of the advantages you get with a traditional IRA and a variable annuity.

As you can see, you gain nothing extra with an annuity, besides fees and charges. (This comparison is not applicable to annuities held in Roth IRAs.)

Can you remind me what the fees and charges you mentioned are?

Yes. In addition to a possible surrender charge if you cash out early, your annuity insurance company will charge you an annual

Traditional IRA vs. Variable Annuity Within an IRA: Which Is Better?

	TRADITIONAL IRA	VARIABLE ANNUITY WITHIN AN IRA
tax deferral	yes	yes
pre-59½ tax penalty	yes	yes
70½ mandatory withdrawal	yes	yes
surrender charges (before about seven years)	no	yes
state premium tax	no	yes
mortality charges	no	yes

mortality fee and expense fees, and that's all on top of any fees associated with the mutual funds you choose. Now, whether paying these fees makes sense, even outside of a retirement account, is something you'll have to decide yourself, but *within* a retirement account, I believe that they are much too hefty a price to pay for a privilege that is already inherent in your retirement account.

Let's look at an example. Say you have two IRAs, each with a $25,000 balance. One is invested in a variable annuity. In this account, you have divided your money equally among five mutual funds. The second account is an IRA but *not* invested in a variable annuity. Here, too, you have $25,000 invested in equal proportions in the same five mutual funds. Let's say that during the next 15 years together those mutual funds average an 8.5 percent annual return. How much will you have in each IRA?

In the first IRA, invested through the variable annuity, you will have $68,976. In the second IRA, invested directly in the mutual funds, you will have $84,994. Why the $16,018 difference? That's the damage the 1.5 percent in annuity-specific fees can do to the growth of your money. And remember, these fees aren't buying you a tax advantage, either, because all your money has been in tax-advantaged retirement accounts.

Finally, don't forget that a variable annuity carries its own early-withdrawal surrender charges on top of the 10 percent IRS penalty tax that applies to both annuities and IRAs.

My financial adviser is recommending that I buy a variable annuity within my retirement account. What should I do?

Get yourself another financial adviser, pronto.

What if I already own a variable annuity in my retirement account?

Unless the variable annuity is an unbelievably great performer, I would advise you to cash it in as soon as the surrender period expires. Take your money and buy into some solid, well-rated, no-load mutual funds within your IRA. If your annuity returns have been horrible, on the other hand, you might want to consider cashing out even if the surrender charge is still in force. Or you could simply withdraw the 10 percent a year you are allowed to take without incurring the surrender penalty and transfer those funds into a good no-load mutual fund; you can do this every year until the surrender period is up. Since the money is already sheltered within a retirement plan, you will not have to worry about the tax implications.

What should I do if my variable annuity is not sheltered within a retirement account?

Everything I noted in the previous answer applies to you, too. But if you're considering cashing out of your annuity altogether, you must also take into account penalties for withdrawals prior to age 59½ *and* ordinary taxation on the money when withdrawn, plus a possible state premium tax. Because of all these pesky factors—the reasons I do not like variable annuities to begin with—I would advise you to see a good, honest fee-based financial planner. Give him or her an exact, detailed description of your financial situation—including your age, your family situation, your financial goals, your assets and liabilities, your tax bracket, the terms of the annuity you purchased, and how long you have owned it. He or she will take these particulars into account and advise you on how to proceed with your contract.

How do I know if a variable annuity is right for me?

In my opinion, it *may* be an advantageous investment only if you like to trade—that is, buy and sell—mutual funds often, won't need your money for years to come, and are in a very high tax bracket now but plan to be in a much lower tax bracket at retirement.

INDEX ANNUITIES

In its effort to keep up with mutual funds, the insurance industry introduced yet another kind of annuity in the mid-1990s—the index annuity. It was created to compete with very popular index funds, mutual funds that track a stock-market index. I have to admit I like the concept—for the right investors.

How does an index annuity work?

Like all annuities, an index annuity is a contract with an insurance company for a specific period of time. An index annuity tracks a particular stock-market index, such as the Standard & Poor's 500. Your rate of return will usually be a set percentage of the increase in that index in the corresponding index year, up to a maximum of a given percent. There is also a guarantee against losses. The surrender period on an index annuity is typically longer than other surrender periods—about seven to ten years.

Can you give me an example of how the set percentages work?

Yes. Let's say that your index annuity promises to give you 50 percent of what the S&P 500 index returns, up to a maximum return of 10 percent per year. You invest $20,000 on March 15. By March 15 of the following year, the S&P 500 index has increased 30 percent. According to the terms of your annuity, the insurance company has to give you 50 percent of that increase, up to a maximum of 10 percent. Since 50 percent of 30 percent is 15 percent, which is 5 percent higher than the preset yearly maximum of 10 percent, you will be credited with a 10 percent gain on your original deposit, in this case $2,000. If the S&P 500 index had gone up only 15 percent for the year, you would be entitled only to a 7.5 percent gain on your investment.

You say there is a guarantee on the downside. What if the S&P 500 goes down 30 percent?

Yes, there is a guarantee on the downside, which is why investors in index annuities accept a ceiling of 10 percent a year on their gains. In fact, for those who do not want to take any downside risk, the index annuity can be a good option. Unlike regular index funds, where you claim 100 percent of the gains but also suffer 100 percent of the decreases, in an index annuity your money can only go up; it cannot go down. If you invest $20,000 in an index annuity on March 15 and by the following March 15 the index has fallen by 30 percent, you will still end up with $20,000 at the end of that year. The next year, when the market rises by 20 percent, you will be credited with 50 percent of that increase up to a maximum of 10 percent or, in this case, 10 percent, or $2,000. So instead of having a total of $18,000 after two years (you would have lost $6,000 in the first year and gained back only $4,000 in the second year), as you would in a typical mutual-fund account, you will have $22,000. This kind of annuity limits your upside but effectively protects you from a downturn.

Please note: This safety feature is not included in all index annuities, so be sure to ask your insurance company whether it applies to the annuity you're considering.

Are there any other safety features attached to index annuities?

Yes. Index annuities typically come with a guarantee as to your total return over the life of the annuity. No matter which available index you choose to track, in the long run you can't lose. Why? Because once your surrender period is over, the insurance company typically guarantees that you will get back at least 110 percent of what you originally invested *or* the balance of your account, whichever is greater. If you invest $20,000, the worst-case scenario will leave you, after seven years, with $22,000, or about a 1.4 percent minimum guaranteed annual return on your investment. Again, if you are willing to give up some upside potential, an index annuity can help you protect yourself against downside risk, both in the short term and the long term.

Are index annuities better in bear or bull markets?

Because of the protections they offer in exchange for limiting upside potential, I like index annuities best in markets that are going down. In a down market, the company has to pay you something even if the indexes plummet. If the indexes go up one year, you can lock in gains for that year. Either way, you avoid taking the hits in the down years.

What would you look out for with an index annuity?

Be sure you know exactly what percentage you'll earn on any increases in the index you choose, as well as the annual and the total maximum and minimum gains. Ask whether the insurance company has the right to change any of these percentages during the contract period. If so, be wary. Finally, be sure you know the length of the surrender period and the size of all fees and sales loads you'll be charged.

How do I know if an index annuity is right for me?

If you do not want to take any risks but still want to play the stock market, a good index annuity may be right for you.

SPLIT ANNUITIES

My financial adviser has put me into a split annuity that gives me monthly income, but he says I will also get all my money back in five years. What is a split annuity, and how is it different from an immediate annuity that is held outside of a retirement account?

A split annuity is a tax-efficient annuity tailored to give you a regular income *plus* growth. In a split annuity, the insurance company simply divides the money you give it into two accounts. One account repays you a designated sum of money each and every month over a specific period of time. The other account is left in place to grow, either through stock-market investments or through accumulated interest payments fixed by the company. The goal is that, by the time the first half of the money is totally depleted through payments to you, the second half will have grown to be worth at least the amount of the original deposit.

The reason people split annuities is this: During the first years, when you are withdrawing money from one half, since you are mainly getting back your principal, you do not have to pay taxes on the majority of the money you are receiving. At the end of the contract, the other half of your annuity is still intact, and you can do it all again. If interest rates are higher or the economy is better than it was during the first contract period, you may do even better the second time around. That is why people like split annuities better than an immediate annuity, where you lock in your income forever at the start.

Are there drawbacks to a split annuity?

It will depend on your goals and on whether the money that you deposit into a split annuity is in a retirement account or not. Outside of a retirement account, in my opinion, in most cases they make no sense whatsoever. This is because you are converting money that you have already paid taxes on slowly but surely to taxable dollars again.

Let's say you deposited $100,000 with money you have already paid taxes on into a split annuity. The annuity company splits that money into two accounts, each with $50,000 in them. You start to receive monthly income from one of those accounts, which makes you very happy—not only are you receiving a higher monthly check than what the interest on the $100,000 could have generated for you, but you also have to pay fewer taxes on those checks because they are made up mainly of your own money coming back to you. All this while the $50,000 on the other side is left to grow back into your original $100,000 by the time the monthly stream of income runs out. And, sure enough, this is exactly what happens. But here is the problem. The $100,000 now in your account is made up of $50,000 of money you paid taxes on, and $50,000 that you have *never* paid taxes on. So if you go to take out that $100,000, you will pay ordinary income tax on $50,000 of it. What if you are in a higher income-tax bracket at that time?

What usually happens, however, is that you do not need the money and you start the process all over again. This time around, you are paying more in taxes on your monthly income, because more of the payment is from money you have never paid taxes on. At the end of the second cycle, *all* $100,000 is taxable if you take it out. What if you then die? Your beneficiaries now owe income tax on all that money. Or what if you need a large sum because you are ill or you want to buy a retirement home or you need to pay to stay in a nursing home? Now you are in trouble. A split annuity can make sense in some cases, such as in a retirement account, where all the money is pretax anyway, but I would check carefully before I signed up for one.

IMMEDIATE, OR INCOME, ANNUITY (SPIA)

What is an immediate, or income, annuity?

An immediate, or income, annuity guarantees the annuitant a fixed income that begins to be paid as soon as the investment is made. This income continues for the rest of his or her life. Also known as an SPIA (single-premium immediate annuity), this is the only type of annuity where you don't incur a 10 percent IRS penalty tax when you take withdrawals before age 59½. In some cases, beneficiaries receive the income from an immediate annuity for a certain period after the death of the annuitant. For the promise of lifelong income, however, you must sign over all the money in the annuity to the insurance company with full knowledge that you will never be able to touch it again.

Are there tax advantages to an immediate annuity?

Yes. If you hold an immediate annuity outside a retirement account, part of each monthly payment is considered a return of principal on which you've already paid taxes, so that portion of the income is not taxed. The return of some of your principal along with the interest your funds are generating creates a higher monthly payment than you could probably get elsewhere on a guaranteed basis. Understand, however, that the higher monthly payment *includes* your principal; with other fixed-return investments, such as CDs or bonds, your principal remains intact.

If you hold an immediate annuity within a retirement account, you have probably purchased the annuity with pretax dollars and so will have to pay income taxes on the entire amount you receive each month.

What determines the amount of monthly income from an SPIA?

The interest portion of the payment is based on the size of your investment, your age, the current interest rates, and the maximum amount of time you have chosen for the company to pay out the stream of income, even if you were to die. The income options range from the highest monthly amounts, for life only, to lower amounts, known as life-plus-five or life-plus-ten years certain.

How do I know if an SPIA is right for me?

Are you looking for a guaranteed monthly income with some tax benefits? Are you someone who immediately needs a higher income than a straight interest-bearing investment can provide? Can you afford to give up access to the principal paid for the annuity? Do you want to take advantage of a high-interest-rate environment? Are you without any beneficiaries? Then an SPIA may make sense for you. The perfect time to have purchased an immediate annuity, for example, with respect to interest rates, would have been in the 1980s, when interest rates were high.

Do you recommend SPIAs?

In most cases, no, because you are giving up all claim to your principal investment. Purchasing an SPIA in a low-interest-rate environment is something I would be especially wary of. If interest rates go up, you are stuck at the lower rate for the rest of your life. In fact, unless interest rates are very high, the rate guarantee tends to work in favor of the insurance company, not you.

TAX-SHELTERED ANNUITIES (TSAs)

Last but not least is the tax-sheltered annuity, or TSA, which many schoolteachers and hospital workers are offered in their retirement plans. The TSA really falls into the category of a retirement plan, since money is invested monthly in a TSA, unlike other annuities that are bought with a lump sum. All the money you invest in a TSA is qualified, or pretax, money—

money on which you haven't yet paid taxes. In most cases, the TSA is an excellent investment vehicle. If you have a TSA in your retirement account, just make sure that the funds are performing in a satisfactory way.

ANNUITIZING YOUR INVESTMENT

When you "annuitize" your investment in an annuity, you agree to receive a fixed monthly income from the insurance company, typically for life. In return, you give up any claim to a lump-sum payment at the end of your original contract with the insurance company—in effect, you hand over all the money in your annuity account to the insurance company forever. Immediate, or income, annuities are set up this way from the beginning; all other kinds of annuities can be converted to this arrangement anytime the owner chooses. The amount of your monthly income is typically based on your age, the amount of your original investment, the current level of interest rates, and the annuitization policy that was part of your original contract.

In some rare cases, annuitization makes sense. But there *are* alternatives. You do not have to annuitize (or even buy an immediate annuity or a split annuity) in order to get monthly income from your annuity. You can simply withdraw money every month from, for example, a single-premium deferred annuity. This way, you are not locked in to a fixed interest rate; you have access to your money or you can leave it to your beneficiaries. But for those who want a guaranteed rate of return and a stable income, here is what you need to know.

I need income from my annuity. How do I decide whether to annuitize or simply take withdrawals?

Unless you want to lock in interest rates that are extremely high and bound to come down *and* the interest rate factors the insurance company uses to figure out your annuity payments are favorable, I would never annuitize. If you need income, just take monthly withdrawals.

LIFE-ONLY OPTION

The most basic annuitization option is called "life only." When you choose this option, the insurance company pays you a designated amount every month, starting immediately, for the rest of your life. The monthly payments tend to be the highest of any of the annuitization options and continue for as long as you live, even if you live a hundred years.

If, on the other hand, you opt for the life-only option and die a month after you start to receive your income, well, too bad— the payments stop, and your heirs get nothing. The reason this option gives you the highest monthly income is that the insurance company knows that once you die, it's off the hook.

How does the insurance company decide how much the monthly payments will be?

Your monthly payout—known as your "income per thousand"— is determined by a number of factors, including your age, your medical history, the size of your investment, and the current interest-rate environment. An insurance company can project your life expectancy with pretty fair accuracy. Still, different companies offer different rates, so it's a good idea to do some research.

I don't understand the term "income per thousand." Can you elaborate?

Yes. Let me use an example. Let's say that you are a 70-year-old man and you enter into a life-only annuity. Based on the insurance company's experience and its trusty actuarial tables, it will assign you a specific monthly income per each $1,000 that you have invested in the annuity. Let's say that you have purchased an annuity worth $100,000 with a single premium. And let's say that the insurance company has agreed to pay you the grand sum of $9.42 per thousand dollars, for the rest of your life. This means that every month the insurance company will pay you $942.

Can you give me an idea of what the current life expectancies are?

Sure. According to the American Council of Life Insurance statistical tables, if you are a 60-year-old man, you are expected to live another 24.6 years. If you are a 60-year-old woman, you are expected to live another 27.4 years. If you are a 65-year-old man, you are expected to live another 20.4 years; a 65-year-old woman is expected to live another 23 years. At age 70, a man's life expectancy is 16.6 years, and a woman's is 18.8 years. If you are a man who has made it to age 75, you are expected to live another 13.2 years. At age 75, a woman is expected to live another 14.9 years.

What happens if the insurance company is wrong and I die sooner than the company expects?

In that case, the insurance company wins, big-time. If you live longer than expected, the insurance company loses. But companies spread their risk over many annuity holders, so it's hardly a financial calamity when some of them outlive the predictions.

What if I fool the insurance company, take good care of myself, and live to be 100 years old?
Then you will get the last laugh. Using the above figures, in which the insurance company is paying you $942 a month, or $11,304 every year, on a $100,000 annuity you bought when you were 70, you would receive $339,120.

So are you saying that I should consider a life-only annuity option only if I can be pretty sure that I will outlive the company's life-expectancy tables?
No, I am not. There is no way to know how long you will live. Your decision should be based on other considerations. If you have a spouse, children, or other people you'd like to take care of after your death, I would avoid this type of annuity like the plague.

LIFE-PLUS-FIVE YEARS CERTAIN OR LIFE-PLUS-TEN YEARS CERTAIN OPTIONS

What is a life-plus-five or life-plus-ten years certain option?
With these annuitization options, the insurance company will pay you a designated amount every month for as long as you live, with one big difference: If you die soon after the payments begin, the annuity will continue monthly payments to your beneficiaries for five or ten years (your choice) from the date of the annuitization contract. In other words, this kind of annuity guarantees income for at least five or ten years *or* for as long as you live, whichever is longer.

What happens if I die the day after I sign up for a life-plus-ten annuity?

Your beneficiaries would get the income you were scheduled to get for the next ten years. If you were to die three years after you started receiving your monthly income, the company would pay your beneficiaries the same monthly amount for seven more years.

Is there any way to renegotiate during the course of my life how much income I will be getting?

No. Once you have chosen an option and start receiving your income, the amount remains the same for the rest of your life and/or for the rest of the time your beneficiaries receive the income. Even if interest rates skyrocket, your fixed income remains the same—fixed. This annuity contract is one that can most easily be compared to a monthly pension from a corporation.

TAXATION OF ANNUITIES

When I take my money out of an annuity, how will I be taxed?

Whether your annuity is qualified or nonqualified, when you withdraw your money from it at age 59½ or older, you will pay ordinary income taxes on any interest or earnings you have received above and beyond your original contribution. If, for example, you purchased a $5,000 annuity, the interest or gains you earned on that $5,000 would be taxable as ordinary income in the year you make your withdrawal. If your annuity is a qualified annuity—that is, if you have purchased it with pre-tax money—you will also pay ordinary income taxes on the original investment portion of your withdrawal.

The manner in which you are taxed on your withdrawals can vary, depending on whether you have a qualified or a nonqualified annuity.

What is the taxation policy on a nonqualified annuity?

Nonqualified annuities that have been purchased after August 13, 1982, are taxed on a Last In, First Out (LIFO) method. Any interest or gains the annuity has earned are considered to have accrued to your account last, and therefore the earnings must come out first—and are treated as taxable income. Once you have withdrawn all your earnings, you can withdraw your original investment without incurring any additional taxes. If you happen to die with money remaining in a nonqualified annuity, your beneficiaries will have to pay income taxes on the earnings when they withdraw the funds.

What is the taxation policy on a qualified annuity?

Since you have never paid taxes on your original investment in a qualified annuity, the original investment and the earnings are both taxable when you (or your beneficiaries) take money out.

Do I pay annual income tax on undistributed earnings on annuities?

No. This is one of the good things about annuities—in fact, it's one of their main selling points. You don't pay taxes on earnings until you withdraw them. As a result, your initial investment tends to grow more quickly than it otherwise would, since not only your principal but also your tax money earns interest or gains. Still, remember: If you withdraw money before age 59½, you will be assessed a 10 percent early-withdrawal fee by the IRS, added to which there may be an insurance company surrender charge.

Besides income tax, is there any other tax I will pay if I take money out of my annuity?

Again, if you're younger than 59½, you may have to pay a 10 percent IRS penalty tax on any earnings you withdraw. There are exceptions; no penalty tax will be in force if you own an immediate annuity or if you take substantially equal periodic payments from the annuity that you have.

I have been told that if I close out the annuity totally, I will owe a state premium tax. What is that?

Very few people know about the state premium tax, but it can certainly take a bite out of your annuity. In many cases, when you close an annuity account (even if you are simply transferring the balance to another company) you will owe a tax in the state in which you originally purchased the annuity. The state tax ranges from about 0.5 percent of your original deposit on a qualified annuity to about 2.5 percent on a nonqualified annuity. In many states, this is the price the state exacts for letting your money grow tax-deferred all these years. Please make sure you ask about a premium tax before buying an annuity in any given state.

What happens if I take my money out of the annuity and then put it directly into a new contract with a different annuity company?

Please don't do this. If you do, you will probably owe ordinary income taxes on anything above your original after-tax contribution, a state penalty tax, and, if you are not at least 59½ years old, a 10 percent IRS penalty tax on your earnings.

What if I leave my annuity to my spouse or children? What taxes will they owe, if any?

If you have purchased a nonqualified annuity (i.e., using after-tax dollars), they will owe ordinary income taxes on any interest or earnings on the account above your original contribution. Say you deposited $25,000 of after-tax money in an annuity, and the annuity is now worth $100,000. If they withdraw all $100,000 at once after your death, they will owe taxes on $75,000, the difference between your original after-tax deposit ($25,000) and how much is in the account when they close it out ($100,000). If you purchased a qualified annuity (i.e., using money you had not yet paid income taxes on), they would owe ordinary income taxes on the entire $100,000.

Do annuities have to go through probate for my beneficiaries to get my money?

No. If you name a beneficiary who survives you, your annuity will avoid probate. If, however, you name your estate as beneficiary, the annuity will probably have to go through probate.

ADDITIONAL RESOURCES

MUTUAL FUNDS

Barron's (weekly)
Dow Jones & Company, Inc.
84 Second Avenue
Chicopee, MA 01020
(800) 369-2834
www.barrons.com

The "Quarterly Mutual Fund Record" provides ten-year statistics: net asset value per share; 12-month dividends from income; and capital-gains distributions (these figures appear in the February, May, August, and November issues).

BusinessWeek (weekly)
P.O. Box 421
Highstown, NJ 08520
(800) 635-1200
www.businessweek.com

The annual mutual funds issue examines the best-performing funds (this usually appears in February).

Smart Money magazine (monthly)
P.O. Box 7538
Red Oak, IA 51591
(800) 444-4204
www.smartmoney.com

In the fall, a special issue generally provides mutual fund statistics and ratings.

Kiplinger's Personal Finance magazine (monthly)
P.O. Box 3292
Harlan, IA 51593
(800) 544-0155
www.kiplinger.com

A special fall issue typically contains detailed mutual fund statistics and rankings.

Forbes (bimonthly)
Forbes, Inc.
60 Fifth Avenue
New York, NY 10011
(800) 888-9896
www.forbes.com

The August or September issue provides statistics and ratings of mutual funds.

The No-Load Fund Investor (monthly)
The No-Load Fund Investor, Inc.
P.O. Box 3029
Brentwood, TN 37024
(800) 706-6364

This newsletter provides model portfolios and extensive data on almost 1,000 no-load mutual funds.

The Individual Investor's Guide to No-Load Mutual Funds
American Association of Individual Investors
625 North Michigan Avenue, Suite 1900
Chicago, IL 60611
(312) 280-0170
www.aaii.com

All AAII members receive a comprehensive book that includes a detailed analysis of no-load mutual funds, including their historical performance, statistical summaries, fund objectives and services, the name of the portfolio manager, and fund addresses and telephone numbers, as well as strategies for winning mutual fund investing. (Please note: The no-load guide is published annually, in March. It is free to members, $19 for each additional member copy; the nonmember price is $24.95.)

Money Magazine (monthly)
P.O. Box 60001
Tampa, FL 33660
(800) 633-9970
www.money.cnn.com

A special issue that appears early in the year provides mutual fund rankings by category.

Morningstar Mutual Funds
Morningstar, Inc.
225 West Wacker Drive
Chicago, IL 60606
(800) 735-0700
www.morningstar.com

Published every other week, and similar to the Value Line stock reports, this invaluable service delivers reports on individual mutual funds.

Mutual Fund Distributions
Internal Revenue Service
Publication #564
(800) 829-3676
www.irs.gov

This IRS publication explains in detail the tax implications for mutual fund ownership, and can be downloaded from the IRS website.

Mutual Fund Fact Book (annual)
Investment Company Institute
1401 H Street NW
Washington, DC 20035
(202) 326-5800
www.ici.org

This book provides ten-year statistical data on some 3,000 mutual funds, broken down by investment objective.

Mutual Fund Sourcebook (annual)
Morningstar, Inc.
225 West Wacker Drive
Chicago, IL 60606
(800) 735-0700
www.morningstar.com

This sourcebook provides performance and risk ratings on load and no-load mutual funds, as well as information on each fund.

Quarterly Low-Load Mutual Fund Update (quarterly)
American Association of Individual Investors
625 North Michigan Avenue, Suite 1900
Chicago, IL 60611
(312) 280-0170
www.aaii.com

This update provides the fund performance of more than 900 no-load and low-load mutual funds by quarter over the last year, as well as over the most recent three- and five-year periods. In addition, the update provides the difference between a mutual fund's performance and that of an average of funds with the same objective, as well as the risk index, yield, and expense ratios. Also included are lists of top-performing funds and the performances of major indexes. With your subscription, you have access to downloads from the website.

Standard & Poor's Stock Guide (monthly)
Standard & Poor's Corporation
55 Water Street
New York, NY 10064
www.standardandpoors.com

This comprehensive stock manual contains some mutual fund information, including net asset value, minimum initial purchase required, maximum sales charge, price record, and yield from investment income.

Other excellent sources include *The Wall Street Journal* and *The New York Times*, as well as most local newspapers, which provide daily and weekly quotes on mutual fund net asset values.

INSURANCE RATING SERVICES FOR ANNUITIES

A. M. Best
(908) 439-2200
www.ambest.com

Duff & Phelps
(312) 263-2610
www.fitchratings.com

Moody's
(212) 553-0300
www.moodys.com

Standard & Poor's
(212) 438-2400
www.standardandpoors.com

CALCULATING YOUR FUND'S COSTS

One of the keys to investing in a mutual fund is figuring out the true inside costs of your fund. This is not the easiest thing to do, because many of the funds are quite good at hiding that information. The site below will help you find the information you need. Also listed are many great sites to help you locate the funds you are looking for, and keep you informed if something happens in a fund you own, as well as advising you on which funds to buy and which ones to sell.

www.personalfund.com

This site provides the most extensive information on fees and the effect they will have on your fund's performance.

www.sec.gov/mfcc/mfcc-int.htm

If you use this site, make sure you have the prospectus of the fund you are interested in handy.

http://biz.yahoo.com/edu/fundcalc.html.

A great source for calculating your fund returns, fees, and taxes.

www.smartmoney.com

This site provides tools to compare mutual funds and select funds based on criteria you choose.

INFORMATION ON THE WEB

www.indexfundsonline.com

This site is a comprehensive resource on index funds and investing.

www.fundalarm.com

Fundalarm keeps track of what is going on in your mutual fund and sends you an alarm to bring important fund news to your attention.

www.ici.org

ICI Mutual Fund Connection is a good place to continue your education of how mutual funds work.

ADDITIONAL RESOURCES

www.vanguard.com

Vanguard is a great educational site on the subject of mutual funds.

www.morningstar.com

A terrific source for mutual fund performance data updated daily, as well as mutual funds news and analysis.

www.mfea.com

The Mutual Fund Education Alliance is an association of no-load fund companies, with a wealth of educational information and manager interviews.

http://biz.yahoo.com/edu/ed_fund.html

The Yahoo! Education Center is a good resource to learn about mutual funds.

BOOKS

Morningstar's Guide to Mutual Funds: 5-Star Strategies for Success by Christine Benz, Peter Di Teresa, and Russel Kinnel. Here you will find everything you need to know about managing fund investments, inside or outside a 401(k).

Common Sense on Mutual Funds: New Imperatives for the Intelligent Investor by John Bogle. This is a book worth checking out on basic information about mutual funds.

INDEX

ABOUT SUZE ORMAN

SUZE ORMAN has been called "a force in the world of personal finance" and a "one-woman financial advice powerhouse" by *USA Today*. A two-time Emmy® Award–winning television show host, *New York Times* best-selling author, magazine and online columnist, writer-producer, and motivational speaker, Suze is undeniably America's most recognized personal finance expert.

Suze has written five consecutive *New York Times* best sellers—*The Money Book for the Young, Fabulous & Broke*; *The Laws of Money, The Lessons of Life*; *The Road to Wealth*; *The Courage to Be Rich*; and *The 9 Steps to Financial Freedom*—as well as the national best sellers *Suze Orman's Financial Guidebook* and *You've Earned It, Don't Lose It*. Her most recent book, *Women & Money*, was published by Spiegel & Grau in February 2007. A newspaper column, also called "Women & Money," syndicated by Universal Press Syndicate, began in January 2007. Additionally, she has created *Suze Orman's*

FICO Kit, *Suze Orman's Will & Trust Kit*, *Suze Orman's Insurance Kit*, *The Ask Suze Library System*, and *Suze Orman's Ultimate Protection Portfolio*.

Suze has written, coproduced, and hosted five PBS specials based on her *New York Times* best-selling books. She is the single most successful fund-raiser in the history of public television, and recently won her second Daytime Emmy® Award in the category of Outstanding Service Show Host. Suze won her first Emmy® in 2004, in the same category.

Suze is contributing editor to *O, The Oprah Magazine* and *O at Home* and has a biweekly column, "Money Matters," on Yahoo! Finance. She hosts her own award-winning national CNBC-TV show, *The Suze Orman Show*, which airs every Saturday night, as well as *Financial Freedom Hour* on QVC television.

Suze has been honored with three American Women in Radio and Television (AWRT) Gracie Allen Awards. This award recognizes the nation's best radio, television, and cable programming for, by, and about women. In 2003, Suze garnered her first Gracie for *The Suze Orman Show* in the National/Network/Sydication Talk show category. She won her second and third Gracies in the Individual Achievement: Program Host category in 2005 and 2006.

Profiled in *Worth* magazine's 100th issue as among those "who have revolutionized the way America thinks about money," Suze also was named one of *Smart Money* magazine's top thirty "Power Brokers," defined as those who have most influenced the mutual fund industry and affected our money, in 1999. A 2003 inductee into the Books for a Better Life (BBL) Award Hall of Fame in recognition of her ongoing contributions to self-improvement, Suze previously received the 1999 BBL Motivational Book Award for *The Courage to Be Rich*. As a tribute to her continuing involvement, in 2002 the organization established the Suze Orman First Book Award to honor a first-time author of a self-improvement book in any category. She received a 2003 Crossing Borders Award from the Feminist Press. The award recognizes a distinguished group of women who not only have excelled in remarkable careers but also have shown great courage, vision, and conviction by forging new places for women in their respective fields. In 2002, Suze was selected as one of five distinguished recipients of the prestigious TJFR Group News Luminaries Award, which honors lifetime achievement in business journalism.

A sought-after motivational speaker, Suze has lectured widely throughout the United States, South Africa, and Asia to audiences of up to fifty thousand people, often appearing alongside individuals such as Colin Powell, Rudy Giuliani, Jerry Lewis, Steve Forbes, and Donald Trump. She has been featured in almost every major publication in the United States and has appeared numerous times on *The View*, *Larry King Live*, and *The Oprah Winfrey Show*.

A Certified Financial Planner®, Suze directed the Suze Orman Financial Group from 1987 to 1997, served as vice president of investments for Prudential Bache Securities from 1983 to 1987, and from 1980 to 1983 was an account executive at Merrill Lynch. Prior to that, she worked as a waitress at the Buttercup Bakery in Berkeley, California, from 1973 to 1980.